Economy and Modern Christian Thought

Theology

Volumes published in this Brill Research Perspectives title are listed at *brill.com/rpth*

Economy and Modern Christian Thought

By

Devin Singh

BRILL

LEIDEN | BOSTON

This paperback book edition is simultaneously published as issue 4.3 (2020) of *Theology*, DOI:10.1163/24683493-12340011.

Library of Congress Control Number: 2022904206

Brill Open Access options can be found at brill.com/openaccess.

Typeface for the Latin, Greek, and Cyrillic scripts: "Brill". See and download: brill.com/brill-typeface.

ISSN 2468-3485
ISBN 978-90-04-51613-7 (paperback)
ISBN 978-90-04-51738-7 (e-book)

This book is printed on acid-free paper and produced in a sustainable manner.

Contents

Economy and Modern Christian Thought

Devin Singh
Department of Religion, Dartmouth College, Hanover, New Hampshire, USA
devin.p.singh@dartmouth.edu

Abstract

This work presents key features of the engagement of Christian theology, ethics, and related disciplines with the market and economic concerns. It surveys ways that the dialogue has been approached and invites new models and frameworks for the conversation. It contends that economy and Christian thought have long been interconnected, and recounts aspects of this relationship and why it matters for how one might engage the economy ethically and theologically. Finally, it highlights a number of sites of emerging research that are in need of development in light of pressing social, political, economic, and conceptual issues raised by modern life, including money, debt, racial capital, social reproduction, corporations, and cryptocurrency.

Keywords

economy – economic – market – theology – ethics – Christian thought – political theology – money – debt – racial capital – social reproduction – cryptocurrency

Introduction

As I finalize the draft of this work, a new wave of the pandemic is upon us.[1] The SARS-CoV-2 Omicron variant surge is taking infection rates to new heights

1 Portions of this research were undertaken while in residence as a visiting fellow at the Center for the Study of Religion, Princeton University and as fellow at the Center of Theological Inquiry, Princeton. Additional portions were supported by the Luce Foundation's Public Theologies of Technology and Presence grant administered through the Institute of Buddhist Studies, Berkeley. I express my thanks to the staff and coparticipants at these institutions for input and support. I have benefitted from research and/or editorial assistance from Gabriela

 | DOI:10.1163/9789004517387_002

around the globe. Of the innumerable concerns and crises engendered by COVID-19, its economic impact has loomed large. Efforts to contain the spread of infection have brought national economies to a near standstill, disrupted global supply chains, and precipitated massive layoffs as companies struggle with reduced cashflow for salaries. As the United States and other nations strove to respond to the initial onslaught of the virus in March 2020, many public voices framed the pandemic's potential impact on the economy along a troubling moral axis: the lives of the vulnerable, particularly the elderly, were weighed against the economic cost of shutdowns and stay-at-home mandates. Promarket pundits prided themselves in putting the economy first, no matter the cost, disingenuously glorifying in their own apparent willingness to die for its sake.[2] The federal government under the Trump administration tacitly agreed, resisting centralized lockdown measures, and attempting to let "market forces" respond to pandemic need.[3] Left to their own devices, each state and local community plotted its own uneasy path mediating between the concerns of protecting the vulnerable and keeping the economic machine moving.

Many were understandably horrified that economic desires might outweigh the value of certain sectors of society. In response, they emphasized the opposite pole over against market pundits, asserting the preferential option for the vulnerable. Still others found the entire calculus and framing itself problematic. Need this be the forced choice, or was it a false dilemma? Were there other ways to approach the challenge morally, economically, and politically? Yet, what is striking to me in this second major surge that threatens to surpass the first is how muted the discussion about this concern has become. Whatever robust moral response there was to the idea of favoring the economy at the expense of the vulnerable appears to have faded. Markets remain open with little discussion now about the potential impact on those who remain vulnerable. Some of this is due no doubt to pandemic fatigue and the depletion of reserves for social, emotional, and moral protest. It is also coupled with the

---

Hull, Caris White, and, in particular, Travis Ables, whose encouragement helped see this project to completion.

2 Perhaps most vociferous was Texas Lt. Gov. Dan Patrick. See, e.g., Jamie Knodel, "Texas Lt. Gov. Dan Patrick Suggests He, Other Seniors Willing to Die to Get Economy Going Again," *NBC News*, Mar 24, 2020, https://www.nbcnews.com/news/us-news/texas-lt-gov-dan-patrick-suggests-he-other-seniors-willing-n1167341.

3 I critiqued what I saw as "market fundamentalism" dictating the administration's response in Devin Singh, "COVID-19 Is Exposing Market Fundamentalism's Many Moral and Practical Flaws," *Washington Post*, April 4, 2020, https://www.washingtonpost.com/outlook/2020/04/10/covid-19-is-exposing-market-fundamentalisms-many-moral-practical-flaws/.

availability of vaccines and the unstated conclusion that those who remain vulnerable do so by choice. While vaccine resistance and misinformation are significant concerns, we know such a conclusion is false in that many remain unvaccinated for a host of legitimate if still troubling reasons.

The pitting of lives against markets and the varying levels of diminishing concern demonstrate the importance of moral and religious reflection on economy. American Christian response during the pandemic, at least in the public eye, focused more on the right to gather in person to worship than about any calling to care for the sick. The moral calculus was framed in terms of staying home and obeying a tyrannical government or defying lockdown orders to demonstrate corporate faithfulness to God.[4] Absent was a different sort of calculus that asked whether enjoying the pleasures of fellowship with other Christians outweighed going out and risking one's life to aid the vulnerable and infected.[5] While solutions to such moral challenges are rarely easy or straightforward, we can improve our personal and corporate responses to such dilemmas by drawing on the thought generated by those who have grappled with similar challenges. We can also find insight from traditions of moral and spiritual discernment that have guided communities across the centuries and consider the examples of their praxis and its outcomes.

The interaction between Christian thought and matters of economy can be traced back through all the traditional demarcations in the development of Christian theology: biblical, apostolic, patristic, medieval, Reformation, early modern, modern, global, and contemporary. The topic reveals links to every conceivable cultural and geographic marker of Christianity. There are well-developed conversations about theology and economics within most of the denominational divisions within the church. Christian theologians and biblical scholars have written extensively on the topic over the preceding centuries. Not only are matters of money, wealth, possessions, and exchange some the most addressed themes in Christian scripture, but sermons, devotional

4 R. R. Reno, "Questioning the Shutdown," *First Things*, March 20, 2020, https://www.firstthings.com/web-exclusives/2020/03/questioning-the-shutdown.

5 Strikingly, Reno did opine about how the fear of death was to blame for lockdowns, but he did not take this in the direction of Christian self-sacrifice for those in need. Rather, he emphasized the importance of choosing certain goods over life preservation: Christians should be like those who "continued to worship, go to musical performances, clash on football fields, and gather with friends." In other words, fear of death should not keep us from social and cultural enjoyments. Reno might have instead explored how the fear of death should not prevent Christians from going out and dying in service to the infected. See R. R. Reno, "Say 'No' to Death's Dominion," *First Things*, March 23, 2020, https://www.firstthings.com/web-exclusives/2020/03/say-no-to-deaths-dominion.

material, and popular reflection on the economy abound within Christian communities, past and present.

This short introductory volume on economy and modern Christian thought provides a selective overview of a very large, diverse, and longstanding field. While I cannot presume to provide a comprehensive map for such vast territory, I illuminate some important sectors as well as provide some key bearing points for broader exploration. In addition to the limitations of my own finitude, interests, and expertise, the constraints of a concise volume induce me to select what I take to be some of the most pressing and thought-provoking concerns at the juncture of Christian thought and economy.

If the conversation between Christianity and economy is millennia old, why do we need such an introduction? There are numerous writings on the subject from a variety of time periods and contexts. We can find longstanding religious concerns about money, wealth, and the use of property, and an ongoing preoccupation with the relationship between the church and wider society on matters that include economic exchange, care of the poor, and just distribution, for instance. Furthermore, just as with topics as broad as theology, religion, or spirituality, every proverbial person on the street has something to say about money and the economy and is prepared to moralize in some way about economic matters. Despite widespread attention to and coverage of the intersection of religion and economics, however, there are important reasons for the introductory overview provided in this work.

First, precisely because we are awash with resources that touch on the topic in some way, we have the need for new guideposts to help orient us. This perennial conversation between Christian thought and economy is in constant flux. The relationship among theology, religious practice, and the economy has been a continual site of reflection, because all three elements in this relation are always changing. Despite the best attempts by conservative impulses, religions change – in their thought systems, forms of common life and practice, and aesthetic and affective senses of what matters most. As religious ideas, actions, and attitudes shift with broader cultural trends, how the economy is understood and engaged also alters. The theological or religious significance of value, labor, money, and exchange is always being rethought. The need for new summations and reframings from the perspectives of Christian thought therefore persists.

Second, just as religious ideas, practices, and institutions are in constant flux, economic practices and institutions, as well as theoretical reflection on the economy, are shifting at breakneck pace. Dwelling as we do in the age of late finance capitalism and the era of global and decentralized capital networks, the financial industry is continually innovating around economic tools and metrics.[6] Collateralized debt instruments such as derivatives and futures, whose failure precipitated the financial crisis of 2008, were themselves relatively recent inventions.[7] The financial crisis, now thirteen years old, set off its own spate of moral reflection on economic concerns. As noted, the COVID pandemic is currently generating its own novel ethical challenges in relation to economy. New economic realities and practices, and the new economic theories and justifications that accompany them, call for new examination and engagement. While assessing and seeking to influence economic matters for two millennia now, Christian thought continues to encounter new economic objects and contexts for analysis.

Third, particularly in our contemporary moment, there has emerged a tendency that exists in some tension with the previous observation of continual flux and change in the economy. With the post – Berlin Wall era and ostensible failure of the socialist experiment came the assertion that "There Is No Alternative" (TINA) to capitalism, a phrase associated with Thatcherism but also espoused in Reaganomics and broader neoliberalism.[8] Rather paradoxically, then, a ponderous cloud proclaiming the immutable endgame of global capital settled onto the conditions of economic change and innovation. Such haze obscures the rapid shifts in economic relations that continue to take place, which suggest possibilities for more radical reconfigurations in economy.[9] Pundit proclamations, such as Francis Fukuyama's concerning the "end of history," celebrated or lamented the supposed new reality concerning the end of change.[10] The waning of state socialist projects raised questions about the condition of liberation theology, for instance, as theological

6 On the "space/time" compression of late capitalism, see David Harvey, *The Condition of Postmodernity: An Enquiry into the Origins of Cultural Change* (Oxford: Blackwell, 1989).

7 For an anthropological analysis of such innovations, see Benjamin Lee and Edward LiPuma, *Financial Derivatives and the Globalization of Risk* (Durham, NC: Duke University Press, 2004).

8 See Claire Berlinski, *"There Is No alternative": Why Margaret Thatcher Matters* (New York: Basic Books, 2008).

9 For an anthropological critique of the totalizing narrative of capital, see Karen Z. Ho, *Liquidated: An Ethnography of Wall Street* (Durham, NC: Duke University Press, 2009); Karen Z. Ho, "Situating Global Capitalisms: A View From Wall Street Investment Banks," *Cultural Anthropology* 20, no. 1 (2005). For one theological take on this narrative, see Devin Singh, "Protest at the Void: Theological Challenges to Capitalist Totality," in *Religion, Protest, and Social Upheaval*, ed. Matthew T. Eggemeier, Peter Joseph Fritz, and Karen V. Guth (New York: Fordham University Press, 2022).

10 Francis Fukuyama, *The End of History and the Last Man* (New York: Free Press, 1992).

reflection on economics struggled to adjust to the new world system.[11] A study such as this, therefore, is important for unmasking ideological presentations of the economy as an inevitability, and for recalling alternative visions and frameworks for change that might upend images of the status quo.

Rather than provide a theological or ethical survey and evaluation of any number of economic concerns – such as poverty, debt, tithing, the prosperity gospel, or labor relations – my primary focus in this work are questions of method and the conceptual challenges of relating economy to Christian thought.[12] I am interested in exploring how and why the two disparate objects and fields can be brought into conversation, and how others have approached such dialogue. In other words, I primarily explore second-order, theoretical frameworks that can justify first-order theological engagement with concrete economic problems. The aim therefore is to equip the reader with a sense of the landscape of approaches to the engagement between Christian thought and economy, to provide a conceptual scaffolding for what makes the engagement theoretically possible, and to trace key trajectories for cutting-edge research at this juncture.

Given my theoretical orientation toward modeling the relation, as the title suggests, my focus is on economy, broadly construed. The aim is to provide a capacious and flexible placeholder for what we might include in this focus. To be sure, economy partly comprises the practices and institutions associated with what is termed "the economy" or "the market," which include material relations of production, exchange, and consumption, and technologies such as money and accounting that support them. Beyond this, my intent is also to signal economy as a concept, as a set of varying ideas around exchange relations and the diverse and often conflicting imaginaries around how such relations might be ordered. My focus on economy certainly also includes "economics," understood as formal reflection and theorizing around economy as a concept and on markets as objects. As we will see, abstractions such as "the economy" or "the market," the general conception of economy, and the discipline of economics all arose in the early modern era. While I review the emergence of

11 Nancy Bedford, "Whatever Happened to Liberation Theology?," *The Christian Century*, Oct. 20, 1999; Ivan Petrella, *The Future of Liberation Theology: An Argument and Manifesto* (Aldershot, UK: Ashgate, 2004); Ivan Petrella, *Beyond Liberation Theology: A Polemic* (London: SCM Press, 2008); Marcella Maria Althaus-Ried, Ivan Petrella, and Luiz Carlos Susin, *Another Possible World* (London: SCM Press, 2007).

12 Readers interested in theological analyses of these and other issues might consider Stefan Schwarzkopf, ed., *The Routledge Handbook of Economic Theology* (London: Routledge, 2020); Paul Oslington, ed., *The Oxford Handbook of Christianity and Economics* (New York: Oxford University Press, 2014).

economics as a scientific discipline in conjunction with the rise of economy in early modernity, however, I refrain here from in-depth engagement with the academic field itself.

In examining the complex relationship between economy and Christianity, I have opted for the expression "Christian thought" over "theology" to indicate that the discourses I draw on transcend the traditional disciplinary divisions between, say, theology versus ethics, or systematic theology versus historical theology. While, in what follows, I survey these various subdisciplinary approaches to the conversation about economy, I do not intend to favor or prioritize one. The catch-all expression "Christian thought" enables an engagement with theological, ethical, philosophical, historical, and practical approaches under the umbrella of Christian reflection on markets, money, exchange, value, and the like. Prioritizing *modern* Christian thought in this study attends to the formation of these various subfields in conjunction with the rise of the market system and economic science.

Furthermore, at least within the American higher educational landscape, the expression "Christian thought" indicates some placement within a religious studies context as opposed to a divinity school, seminary, or other confessional or religious professional setting, where the term "theology" is used with less ambivalence. This signals that I do not attempt to set out a normative theological position about what the relation between Christian thought and economy *should* be in light of doctrinal or confessional commitments. My approach instead attempts to be primarily descriptive rather than prescriptive. Undoubtedly, however, my political and theological allegiances, including those that may remain implicit and opaque even to me, influence such an inquiry. While I mostly refrain from direct adjudication between the various perspectives and approaches included here, no doubt my subject position influences what I have selected and how I present it.

Such subjectivity includes the filters of my existence as a cisman in a brown-skinned body of South Asian and Anglo-American descent, whose formative, early childhood years were spent in Africa. I do not have a good shorthand way to help explain what this atypical amalgamation entails, nor are there communities to which I can easily refer that might serve as ideal types to summarize the peculiarities of my outlook. My interests and intuitions have been shaped by growing up in an international development context, where my mother, who raised me on her own, served as a US foreign service officer charged with managing aid projects in Cameroon and Morocco. As such, I accompanied her frequently on site visits to agricultural and industrial programs, health and educational initiatives, and other locations of social, political, and economic involvement in the form of American aid. Such projects and my associated experiences typically were situated at the complex nexus of European colonial legacy, anti- and neocolonialism, American interventionism, native nationalisms, identity politics, soft power, militarism, structural adjustment, benevolent paternalism, Christian missionization, and a host of other national and international interests, combined with economic need and desire for help as well as suspicion and resistance on the part of recipient nations.

Experiencing such complexities and tensions firsthand on the ground has led me generally to eschew swift programmatic recommendations, doctrinaire claims of positional supremacy, or easy denunciations of ideological adversaries. Mediating two sets of already composite ethnicities within my body and straddling vast cultural divides internationally has forged in me the desire to bring diverse conversations and viewpoints together, not necessarily for reconciliation and synthesis but often for productive disruption and unexpected insight. The many dislocations of my own identity and life journey have tuned me in to the surprise wisdom that can emerge from juxtaposition and apparent contradiction. All these factors influence my topical selection for this study as well as the methods of mediation and exchange among divergent fields of study. They mean that some of the themes I bring into dialogue may be jarring, that I try to disrupt binaries and clear separations between opposing fields or issues, and that tidy resolutions and firm categorizations may be deferred.

My positionality also includes a vexed relationship to confessional and organized Christianities, with simultaneous attraction to and repulsion from Christianity's past and present manifestations. My persistence in engaging and valuing theological discourse while striving to discipline it within social scientific frameworks reflects the ambivalences of my biography that straddles the worlds of theology and religious studies (and social science more broadly). My early exposure to geopolitical realities took a specific direction when, as an undergraduate, I found myself working through my belief system and drawn powerfully to religious discourses around economics, social and political struggle, and questions of identity. In other words, Christian thought provided one key matrix for me to sort through and mobilize my formative childhood experiences, identity struggles, and emerging political concerns.

I pursued these interests both academically and practically through divinity school, nonprofit and ministry work, community development, and further graduate study in religion and in social theory. I had deep existential and activist concerns about economic and racial injustice, which I sought to mediate with highly theoretical and abstract discussions around the epistemology of money and finance, the semiotics of currency, and the institutions of political sovereignty. The idiosyncrasies of this identity, biography, and research are refracted here in a study that also resists denominational affiliation and confessional conformity, mediates abstract theory and practical concerns, and attempts to do justice to the complexity and nuance of the material by resisting reduction and simplification. The upshot is a study that I hope presents the issues in a new light and offers readers a fresh take on matters of perennial concern in a way that can inform further research as well as praxis.

In what follows, I first survey a variety of approaches to the dialogue between economy and Christian thought. The aim is to provide the reader with a sense of the landscape of engagement and offers one way of organizing the field. The approaches I review follow typical field distinctions within theology and religious studies and mark one way to think about the conversation. These tried and true, but now increasingly transgressed, boundary markers also provide a launching point for new work to move beyond such limited frameworks.

The second part explores why the relation between the economy and Christian thought should not be taken for granted, and why modeling and articulating the relation is something I take to be central to good work in this dialogue. I favor a genealogical approach that seeks to expose longstanding links between Christianity and economy. In other words, one of the key contributions I hope to make is to show how Christian and economic thought are interwoven and specifically how the rise of the modern economy was theologically motivated and informed. Such a relation presents challenges for thinking theologically about economic reform or resistance, even as it forms the possibility for such intervention.

The third and final part is devoted to surveying key trajectories of inquiry at the intersection of economy and modern Christian thought, many of which are still nascent and in need of further development. These are sites of social and political import, and present exciting horizons for future research. They are also a sampling of many possible routes for inquiry as this important dialogue between economy and modern Christian thought continues.

1 Approaches

This part surveys a variety of ways scholars have approached the matter of Christian thought in relation to the economy. I explore what I term scriptural, social-scientific, ethical, philosophical, and theological approaches, explaining what is distinctive about each and noting some characteristic studies. My descriptions include forms of disciplinary framing of the priorities and questions each asks, as well as the aims and outcomes generated by such studies.

Such traditional disciplinary distinctions within Christian thought are one way to begin to outline the terrain of the conversation with economy, acknowledging that there are different emerging modes of engagement.

These categories loosely map onto typical departmental or subfield differentiations in many modern, Western religious studies departments or divinity schools. This part is retrospective in nature and uses this well-worn template as a way to frame the work that has already been done. However, there is much justified call for transdisciplinary engagement and even a movement beyond these subfields. Both the external pressures of neoliberal capitalism in the form of funding cuts, departmental consolidation, and administrative reconfiguration of fields, as well as internal challenges to and dismantling of canonicity and Eurocentric frameworks of knowledge making, mean that these subfields are under transformation if not erosion. It remains to be seen what the future holds, but the third part of this study will highlight areas of potential thematic focus for further research.

My intention is not to issue a value judgment about which of these subfield approaches is preferable and I must stress that it is rare to find one approach deployed in a pure or totalizing manner. Typically, scholars will draw from and incorporate a variety of methods, even if one approach is dominant. The lines between, say, theology and ethics are often blurred, and many ethicists engage in theological ethics in a way not easily distinguished from systematic theology. But these quandaries attend any attempt at classification of subfields within religious studies or theology as umbrella disciplines, and are thus not barriers to inclusion here. Furthermore, the following classifications are ideal types that may be helpful for students of the field to map the various ways one can study Christian thought and economy. Transgressing the boundaries of these types and creating new vantage points are also potential paths for innovation. Before we can subvert and deconstruct, however, it helps to know something about what has come before, in order to have a sense of that which we are reconfiguring. This part also raises questions of method that will accompany us throughout this study. As we will see, a number of conceptual and methodological challenges emerge in the attempt to bring these realms of Christian thought and economy into conversation.

1.1 *Scriptural*

Scriptural or biblical approaches are those that seek to mine the Bible for commentary and insights on economic matters, typically making sacred scripture the centerpiece of the study and offering it as an authoritative word for evaluation and intervention. Generally, the Bible, taken as the word of God or as an otherwise authoritative basis for prescription, is the control mechanism that generates the patterns and guidelines to which one should conform in terms of economic values, market behavior, or policy considerations. These approaches may be more or less scholarly in their form; they may include biblical exegesis of varying degrees of critical distance, and might engage biblical commentaries and even other biblical scholars and so-called biblical theologians. Other examples may be intended for personal devotional use or as self-help manuals for spiritual growth. We can include in this category everything from tracts and handbooks showing the "biblical principles" for money management and prosperity, for instance, to biblical reflections on the "godly" and righteous use of one's wealth, or injunctions toward simplicity, almsgiving, and poverty based upon scriptural witness.[13]

These methods are often seen in the proof-texting approaches of fundamentalist or evangelical scholars but may also include liberal or mainline Protestant and Catholic approaches that believe one can discern a clear biblical blueprint for the relationship between Christian thought and economics. They may not be *biblicist* in a strict sense, but authors do not use much more than their own reflection on biblical passages, or the reflection of other authorities on biblical passages, to distill what they take as principles for Christian economic comportment. Thus, these approaches view the dialogue between Christian thought and economy in a rather unmediated way. One can discern a straightforward meaning of a biblical passage, and enjoin a believer to live out that principle individually or communally in response to some economic situation. Mediated through the life of the believer and community, and supported by the Holy Spirit, this biblical insight should then have impact upon the world.

One way that conservative and liberal approaches often diverge is that conservatives will establish biblically based criteria for individual economic behavior, whereas the liberal frameworks may use biblical arguments for policy proposals and social change at the communal and structural levels. Stereotypically, the conservative approach regards liberty as a primary virtue, individualistically construed. This often excludes consideration of how the economy has been constructed, thus missing attention to preceding history as well as to systems or laws, except in the case of enjoining the government to protect individual freedoms. Liberal approaches certainly have a category for individual or personal sin, but also extend analysis to themes of structural or systemic sin and evil. The liberal emphasis on communal responsibility

---

13 Ronald J. Sider, *Rich Christians in an Age of Hunger: A Biblical Study*, 2nd ed. (Downers Grove, IL: InterVarsity Press, 1984); Craig L. Blomberg, *Neither Poverty nor Riches: A Biblical Theology of Material Possessions* (Grand Rapids: Eerdmans, 1999).

and care for the neighbor, particularly the vulnerable or marginal neighbor, trumps – rhetorically, at least – self-focused or individualistic concerns.[14]

Again, regardless of the ends toward which an interpretation is put, this approach makes reading and interpreting biblical passages the centerpiece. It uses varying types of hermeneutical lenses, such as plain sense, reader response, or historical-critical, to establish "what the Bible says" about an economic matter. It then constructs proposals for what the lives of believers or society should look like as a result.

1.2 *Social-Scientific*

This admittedly broad category captures social-scientific or socio-theoretical approaches that could be further described as primarily historical, sociological, or anthropological. Such studies may appear as interventions in these respective fields or as works of religious studies. Such studies often document and analyze a particular set of relations between religious thought and practice, on one hand, and economic ideas and formations, on the other. The subject matter may include theological discourse as one of the sites of analysis. The purpose of such writing may not be to construct theological systems, ethical norms, or philosophical concepts, although such works may engage and even make use of them as part of their analyses. Rather, the purpose may be to contribute to a thick description of a particular historical or social context or conceptual assemblage, in order to aid in understanding the context in question. One may engage in social-scientific study of the Bible as a historical document, for instance, using archaeology and other ancient texts to establish a window onto economic patterns in a particular period, without centering the Bible as authoritative scripture and using it as a springboard for a normative project, as in the case of the previous approach.

Examples of this type of work can take many forms, as diverse as the fields mentioned. Roland Boer's work on the political economy of ancient Israel and the Levant, using Historical Marxist and Annales School methods, is one clear example of engaging the Bible social scientifically while not centering it authoritatively.[15] There is also a well-developed conversation among scholars

---

14 These liberal and conservative dichotomies of course leave much to be desired, and examples can be found that transgress this simple characterization. One example of a more evangelical and biblically based approach that does examine structural sin is Stephen Charles Mott, *Biblical Ethics and Social Change*, 2nd ed. (New York: Oxford University Press, 2011).

15 Roland Boer, *The Sacred Economy of Ancient Israel*, Library of Ancient Israel (Louisville, KY: Westminster John Knox Press, 2015).

of the New Testament and ancient Christianity around Greco-Roman economy as well as economic claims and practices of early Christian communities.[16] One might here also include much of Peter Brown's oeuvre, documenting as he does in rich detail the relations between Christianity and late antique economy.[17] Of the numerous important studies of medieval economies, Jacques Le Goff and Odd Langholm each document the scholastic attitudes toward usury, markets, money, and other forms of exchange.[18] Natalie Zemon Davis's classic study of the shifts in understanding around gift giving in sixteenth-century France and Switzerland, for instance, provides rich insights into the relation between theology and economics at the pivotal historical juncture of the Protestant Reformation.[19] Michael Welker and Jürgen von Hagen have edited an important and highly original collection of historical, legal, sociological, and ethical interventions around Christianity and money.[20] Such studies provide insights on how the intersection of Christian thought and ecclesial practice with economic ideas and institutions might impact subsequent social formations in terms of religiously coded economies of exchange. They are historically descriptive approaches that attend to the centrality of religion in economic principles and practices, and to the ways economy shapes and influences religion.

---

16 E.g., Bruce W. Longenecker and Kelly D. Liebengood, eds., *Engaging Economics: New Testament Scenarios and Early Christian Reception* (Grand Rapids, MI: Eerdmans, 2009); Thomas R. Blanton and Raymond Pickett, eds., *Paul and Economics: A Handbook* (Minneapolis: Fortress Press, 2017); Jennifer A. Quigley, *Divine Accounting: Theo-Economics in Early Christianity*, Synkrisis (New Haven, CT: Yale University Press, 2021).

17 Peter Brown, *Poverty and Leadership in the Later Roman Empire*, The Menahem Stern Jerusalem Lectures (Hanover, NH: University Press of New England, 2002); Peter Brown, *Through the Eye of a Needle: Wealth, the Fall of Rome, and the Making of Christianity in the West, 350–550 AD* (Princeton, NJ: Princeton University Press, 2012).

18 Jacques Le Goff, *Your Money or Your Life: Economy and Religion in the Middle Ages*, trans. Patricia Ranum (New York: Zone Books, 1998); Jacques Le Goff, *Money and the Middle Ages: An Essay in Historical Anthropology* (Cambridge: Polity, 2012); Odd Langholm, *Economics in the Medieval Schools: Wealth, Exchange, Value, Money and Usury according to the Paris Theological Tradition, 1200–1350* (Leiden: Brill, 1992); Odd Langholm, *The Merchant in the Confessional: Trade and Price in the Pre-Reformation Penitential Handbooks* (Leiden: Brill, 2003).

19 Natalie Zemon Davis, *The Gift in Sixteenth-Century France* (Madison: University of Wisconsin Press, 2000).

20 Jürgen von Hagen and Michael I. Welker, eds., *Money as God? The Monetization of the Market and the Impact on Religion, Politics, Law, and Ethics* (Cambridge: Cambridge University Press, 2014).

Noteworthy in this category is a cluster of studies around the emergence of capitalism and the role that theology and religious belief and practice played in this process. Such inquiries have shaped my own understanding of the imbrications of modern economy with Christian thought, links that are, as I have noted, a central concern of this work. Landmark studies include those by Max Weber, R. H. Tawney, and Albert Hirschman, which consider broad societal trends and religious movements.[21] These approaches employ historical sociology and political theory to present the interaction between theological doctrine and the economic activity of believers or societies affected by believing communities. Other studies center around the environments and thought life of key economic thinkers, such as Pierre Nicole or Adam Smith, both instrumental thinkers in the development of market society who utilized theological concepts in making their claims.[22] Still other studies, such as those by Kathryn Lofton, Bethany Moreton, and George González, may consider a particular theme such as consumerism or media influence, or institutions such as corporations, and assess the forms of religious belief or ritual that subsist in ostensibly secular business practices, or ask how such practices display attributes that could be categorized as religious.[23]

21 Max Weber, *The Protestant Ethic and the Spirit of Capitalism*, trans. Stephen Kalberg, rev. and updated ed. (New York: Oxford University Press, 2011); R. H. Tawney, *Religion and the Rise of Capitalism: A Historical Study* (London: Verso, 2015); Albert Hirschman, *The Passions and the Interests: Political Arguments for Capitalism Before its Triumph* (Princeton, NJ: Princeton University Press, 1977).

22 Paul Oslington, ed., *Adam Smith as Theologian* (New York: Routledge, 2011); Paul Oslington, *Political Economy as Natural Theology: Smith, Malthus and Their Followers* (London: Routledge, 2018); Lisa Hill, "The Hidden Theology of Adam Smith," *European Journal of History of Economic Thought* 8, no. 1 (2001); David Singh Grewal, "The Political Theology of *Laissez-Faire*: From *Philia* to Self-Love in Commercial Society," *Political Theology* 17, no. 5 (2016); Benjamin M. Friedman, *Religion and the Rise of Capitalism* (New York: Alfred A. Knopf, 2021); Harvey Cox, *The Market as God* (Cambridge, MA: Harvard University Press, 2016).

23 Bethany Moreton, *To Serve God and Wal-Mart: The Making of Christian Free Enterprise* (Cambridge, MA: Harvard University Press, 2009); Kevin Michael Kruse, *One Nation under God: How Corporate America Invented Christian America* (New York: Basic Books, 2015); George J. González, *Shape-Shifting Capital: Spiritual Management, Critical Theory, and the Ethnographic Project* (Lanham, MD: Lexington Books, 2015); Kathryn Lofton, *Consuming Religion* (Chicago: University of Chicago Press, 2017); James Dennis LoRusso, *Spirituality, Corporate Culture, and American Business: The Neoliberal Ethic and the Spirit of Global Capital* (New York: Bloomsbury Academic, 2017); Daniel Vaca, *Evangelicals Incorporated: Books and the Business of Religion in America* (Cambridge: Harvard University Press, 2019); Emily Beth Hill, *Marketing and Christian Proclamation in Theological Perspective* (Lanham, MD: Lexington Books/Fortress Academic, 2021).

Another school of thought that bears mention here uses economic principles and frameworks to analyze religious belief and participation. Works by Rodney Stark and Laurence Iannaccone are examples of this method.[24] While the dialogue is rarely one between theology and economics at a conceptual level per se, this approach, often dubbed the "economics of religion," shows the impact of economic models on sociological frameworks that are then used to analyze religious claims and movements. Here, the site of interaction is the use of economically informed models of social decision-making, based on rational choice utility theory, to analyze choices made by religious actors or the socio-economic viability of belief-informed actions in the world. Such religious actors are viewed as consumers making rational economic decisions as the basis of belief and practice.

The "economics of religion" frameworks scrutinize theological efficacy according to market principles as defined by neoclassical economic theory. Good doctrine in such cases is that which conforms to principles of efficiency and productivity, for instance, or provides supply where there is demand. Such economic principles also explain the success, spread, or impact of a set of beliefs. A free or regulated "market" in religion, within which actors make such utility-maximizing decisions, is one explanatory principle marshalled. The success and eventual decline of the Catholic church during medieval Christendom, for instance, can be explained by a theory of monopoly, in which the new Protestant sects were market disruptors exploiting unaddressed needs of believers, understood here as consumers and purchasers in a faith market.[25] Such models can be persuasive from the standpoint of rational choice, and often have the ring of common sense due to the ways many in American and European contexts are immersed in such rational choice reasoning. But these studies are rarely illuminating or explanatory, often serving to vindicate utility theory by showing how empirical data on religious movements might fit into the given economic framework.[26]

---

24 Rodney Stark and Roger Finke, *Acts of Faith: Explaining the Human Side of Religion* (Berkeley: University of California Press, 2000); Laurence Iannaccone and William S. Bainbridge, "Economics of Religion," in *The Routledge Companion to the Study of Religion*, ed. John Hinnells (London: Routledge, 2010).

25 Robert B. Ekelund Jr., Robert F. Hébert, and Robert D. Tollison, "The Political Economy of the Medieval Church," in *The Oxford Handbook of the Economics of Religion*, ed. Rachel M. McCleary (Oxford: Oxford University Press, 2011).

26 On the critique of rational choice theory as not explanatory but aimed rather at self-vindication, see Ian Shapiro, *The Flight from Reality in the Human Sciences* (Princeton, NJ: Princeton University Press, 2005).

1.3 *Ethical*

What I am terming ethical approaches are those concerned with creating moral frameworks for evaluating the relation between Christian thought and economy. Typically they are also intended to influence the market and economic behavior through religious-ethical frameworks and principles. Such approaches may (and usually do) use biblical and theological themes and sources, but center on various ethical traditions and theories. Such ethical theories may be theologically informed to varying degree, but need not be distinctively Christian. Such theoretical dialogue partners include narrative ethics, virtue ethics, deontology, utilitarianism, feminist and womanist ethics, intersectionality theory, and critical race theory. Correct thought and conduct and themes such as responsibility, justice, freedom, and moral culpability or exoneration, are typical preoccupations. The emphasis is on establishing a consistent and coherent ethical system to undergird and justify economic interventions, more than it is an extended preoccupation with the theological images and doctrine that may be invoked. Such ethical approaches may draw on ethical principles and frameworks from different historical periods.

Thinkers exemplifying an ethical approach are secondarily concerned with the theological systems at play, and generally take up one or two theological principles or loci, such as God's love or justice, if they do engage theology explicitly. They then take these theological principles and develop an ethical stance on economic relations in conversation with other ethicists and frameworks. In this sense, the distinction between ethical approaches and theology aligns with the established (although always contested) line between religious ethics and theology as subdisciplines. Characteristically, the former is concerned with building and evaluating structures of moral inquiry while the latter is concerned with describing and analyzing relations among points of doctrine. While some ethical engagements may draw substantially upon theological material, their categorization as ethical is a matter of their preoccupation. Although there is important overlap, the disciplinary emphases are different, and this distinction transfers into the realm of economic engagement.

Notable recent examples of ethical engagement with economy include D. Stephen Long's work on retrieving alternative or emergent traditions of Christian social teaching around economic ethics.[27] Lisa Cahill has intervened in a variety of ethical concerns, including those of economic justice, drawing

27 D. Stephen Long, *Divine Economy: Theology and the Market* (London: Routledge, 2000); D. Stephen Long, Nancy Ruth Fox, and Tripp York, *Calculated Futures: Theology, Ethics, and Economics* (Waco, TX: Baylor University Press, 2007).

on Catholic and broader Christian social teaching.[28] William Cavanaugh has offered reflection on matters of consumption and market values informed by his own work in Christian ethics and Catholic thought.[29] While Cavanaugh assumes a critical stance toward capitalism, Michael Novak marshalled Catholic and broader Christian principles toward a theological and ethical defense of capitalism and free market systems.[30] Mary Hirschfeld plots a mediating, if still critical, engagement with modern economics from a Thomistic perspective informed by natural law traditions.[31] Reformed thinkers such as Max Stackhouse draw on nuances of their tradition to construct Christian ethical responses to globalization and economic policy.[32]

Still other contemporary ethicists have drawn on labor theory, concerns about global financial markets, as well as racial and gender justice to complexify Christian ethical evaluations of economy. Joerg Rieger's work consistently sets Christian thought into conversation with an analysis of labor movements and grassroots protest to challenge ethical limitations of capitalism.[33] Nimi Wariboko has assessed the global financial system in dialogue with theological and ethical principles for a just world order, one that allows fuller participation by the Global South.[34] Ilsup Ahn has evaluated debt relations with a particular eye to the impact of indebtedness on marginalized communities, using Christian ethical principles of just exchange to challenge predatory lending practices.[35] Keri Day has issued an ethical challenge to neoliberalism drawing on womanist thought and theology.[36]

---

28 Lisa Sowle Cahill, *Global Justice, Christology and Christian Ethics* (New York: Cambridge University Press, 2013).

29 William T. Cavanaugh, *Being Consumed: Economics and Christian Desire* (Grand Rapids, MI: Eerdmans, 2008).

30 Michael Novak, *The Catholic Ethic and the Spirit of Capitalism* (New York: Free Press, 1993). For Protestant and evangelical defenses of the free market, see, e.g., Humberto Belli and Ronald H. Nash, *Beyond Liberation Theology* (Grand Rapids, MI: Baker, 1992); David Chilton, *Productive Christians in an Age of Guilt-Manipulators: A Biblical Response to Ronald J. Sider*, 3rd ed. (Tyler, TX: Institute for Christian Economics, 1985).

31 Mary L. Hirschfeld, *Aquinas and the Market: Toward a Humane Economy* (Cambridge, MA: Harvard University Press, 2018).

32 Max L. Stackhouse et al., *God and Gobalization*, 4 vols. (Harrisburg, PA: Trinity Press International, 2000).

33 Joerg Rieger, *No Rising Tide: Theology, Economics, and the Future* (Minneapolis, MN: Fortress Press, 2009).

34 Nimi Wariboko, *God and Money: A Theology of Money in a Globalizing World* (Lanham, MD: Lexington Books, 2008).

35 Ilsup Ahn, *Just Debt: Theology, Ethics, and Neoliberalism* (Waco, TX: Baylor University Press, 2017).

36 Keri Day, *Religious Resistance to Neoliberalism: Womanist and Black Feminist Perspectives* (New York: Palgrave Macmillan, 2016).

1.4 *Philosophical*

The philosophical approach draws on philosophical and critical theory as primary conversation partners with religious perspectives to approach economic concerns. For our purposes, I am concerned with those that use the Christian tradition as an angle of assessment. While these approaches engage in ethical reflection and issue ethical imperatives, the emphasis is on analyzing and clarifying systems of thought. The aim is not primarily to develop a completely fleshed-out ethical system or set of policy proposals for moral action in the world, but to assess, challenge, and transform conceptual systems that bear on economic matters and draw from or speak to religious points of view.

These approaches may be distinguished from more properly theological methods in that they draw substantially on philosophical voices and are less beholden to parameters such as faithfulness to a perceived tradition or sacred scripture, body of doctrine or set of doctrinal loci, or a particular confessional community. Such philosophical sources also typically appeal to reason or experience over forms of special revelation, which remain legitimate sources for theology. The boundaries between what counts as philosophy or theology are regularly blurred, and many approaches move fluidly between the two. Given the centuries of discursive proximity between philosophy and theology in the West this can be expected.

One's stance on this boundary between philosophy and theology, as well as on the legitimacy of (often secular) philosophical voices, determines to what degree one views a philosophical approach as an acceptable method for engaging economics from a religious perspective. For example, biblical approaches often attempt to construct models for and normative stances toward economic concerns in an unmediated fashion, eschewing dialogue with philosophical voices under the guise of a "plain sense" reading of scripture. Such an approach gains its legitimacy and authority through appeals to "direct" or "common sense" interpretations of biblical passages in a way that can claim the full authority of the Bible as God's word without being filtered through ostensibly "worldly" philosophical discourse. Some theological projects may proceed similarly, attributing to theology a status as quasi-special revelation, with a better purchase on the truth than philosophy and hence better equipped to analyze and engage economy.

Such approaches are no less mediated by human nature and social context, and are no less philosophically informed. Authors simply refrain from raising such assumptions and interpretive lenses to the foreground for interrogation, allowing them to operate implicitly. This is why philosophical approaches may appear to be preoccupied with interpretive matters and questions of hermeneutics. Being aware of the theoretical mediation that attends any act of reading, interpretation, and articulation of propositions and norms, no matter how apparently commonsensical, means taking care to explain the sources, benefits, and pitfalls of one's chosen framework. Consideration of one's contextual influences, theoretical lenses, and even economic predispositions can be helpful when analyzing economy.

Among examples of philosophical approaches, Paul Oslington surveys early modern philosophy and natural theology for its contributions to economic thinking. He sheds light on Adam Smith's theological presuppositions as well as the philosophical concerns undergirding Smith's moral and economic pronouncements.[37] Adam Kotsko assesses more recent history, examining the origins and ascendancy of neoliberalism from a political-theoretical and philosophical viewpoint, while drawing on religious reflection on demonization to make sense of this economic system's moral and rhetorical force.[38] Joshua Ramey explores how neoliberal approaches to economy evince the desire to mitigate contingency and risk, and he draws on studies of divination practices to evaluate and critique such attempts.[39] Philip Goodchild contends in *Theology of Money* that modern monetary systems themselves reveal an implicit theology, and he explores this in terms of principles such as the faith that sustains the global credit system.[40] Goodchild devotes primary attention to explicating and problematizing the thought systems, assumptions, and values undergirding modern money or the patterns of desire under capitalism. From there he offers normative ethical statements and visions, such as his belief in the corrosiveness of modern faith in an abstract credit system as opposed to faith and trust in communal relations. Goodchild's recent magnum opus, a trilogy titled *Credit and Faith*, takes a step beyond a philosophical analysis of economy by probing the symbiotic relationship between philosophy and economy, asking how both might be transcended and reimagined because of this relationship and the tensions it raises.[41] My own work straddles social-scientific and

37 Oslington, *Political Economy*.

38 Adam Kotsko, *Neoliberalism's Demons: On the Political Theology of Late Capital* (Stanford: Stanford University Press, 2018).

39 Joshua Alan Ramey, *Politics of Divination: Neoliberal Endgame and the Religion of Contingency* (Lanham, MD: Rowman & Littlefield, 2016).

40 Philip Goodchild, *Theology of Money* (Durham NC: Duke University Press, 2009).

41 Philip Goodchild, *Credit and Faith* (Lanham, MD: Rowman & Littlefield, 2020); Philip Goodchild, *Economic Theology: Credit and Faith II* (Lanham, MD: Rowman & Littlefield, 2020); Philip Goodchild, *The Metaphysics of Trust: Credit and Faith III* (Lanham, MD: Rowman & Littlefield, 2021).

philosophical approaches, but tends toward the conceptual and theoretical in a way that situates it within this category as well.[42]

1.5 *Theological*

Theological approaches to the economy relate specific points of Christian doctrine to economic practices, themes, and concerns. Theological reflection on economics has emerged from various denominational traditions such as Catholicism, Eastern Orthodoxy, and Protestantism; theological movements such as liberationist, public, feminist, Womanist, Black, Asian American, Indigenous, Latinx, and Radical Orthodox; and geographically contextual theologies from Africa, Asia, North and South America, and Europe. As distinguished from the foregoing methods, theological approaches primarily explore theological concepts, often systematically, and then delineate the implications of their interpretations for the theological systems in question and for economic structures in light of new theological insights. This rapprochement is guided by the view that core Christian doctrines about God, creation, humanity, salvation, ecclesiology, and so forth are relevant to economic exchange, modes of production, market structures, ideas of value, and the like.

Such projects may construct theological models in order to offer an exhortation toward specific economic policy and behavior. Peruvian theologian Gustavo Gutiérrez asks, for instance, what the "God of life" means for the living death faced by the masses of the world's poorest and what the church must do in response.[43] He advances a vision for what he takes to be the flourishing of life among such vulnerable communities, charging Christians and all people of good will toward such pursuits. Other studies might survey how various theologians have imagined economic relations in light of biblical and theological tradition. Leonardo Boff examines the life and teachings of St. Francis of Assisi, for instance, to retrieve theological principles to address economic injustice in the service of liberation.[44]

Liberation theology deserves pride of place as the modern theological tradition par excellence that has made economic analysis a guiding concern, and that has spurred such reflection in other theological traditions in response. While a broad and diverse category, liberation theology is marked by using socio-analytic tools to consider problems and shortcomings in economic

42 Devin Singh, *Divine Currency: The Theological Power of Money in the West* (Stanford: Stanford University Press, 2018).

43 Gustavo Gutiérrez, *The God of Life*, trans. Matthew J. O'Connell (Maryknoll, NY: Orbis, 1991).

44 Leonardo Boff, *Francis of Assisi: A Model for Human Liberation* (Maryknoll, NY: Orbis, 2006).

systems and then drawing upon theological tradition to conceptually confront economic injustice and to motivate praxis. Centrally operative is the theological concept of God's "preferential option for the poor," a claim derived from biblical sources and the Catholic magisterium that describes divine solidarity with the poor and marginalized over and against individuals and systems that exploit them.[45] From this core principle other divine attributes, such as divine love or wrath, may be rethought. The principle also provides a lens for interpreting biblical accounts such as the exodus and Gospel narratives of Jesus's actions. Values such as God's will for justice for the poor, liberation for the oppressed, and the correction of systemic sin and evil are elaborated upon from scripture and further theological reflection. Liberation theologians offer models of a liberating God on the side of the poor, and of a faithful church that seeks to imitate such divine solidarity with the "least of these" (Matthew 25:40). They then juxtapose these models to opposing economic systems, advancing new visions for ecclesial community, public life, and politics.

Protestant variants exist, but liberation theology emerged within Catholic contexts and can be understood in relation to a broader body of work known as Catholic Social Teaching (CST). While the Catholic church can rightly point to expressions of social, economic, and political concern over its entire existence, CST is a label applied to a modern conversation on socio-economic issues that began in the late nineteenth century.[46] With the rise of industrialization, the emergence of the capitalist market system, the coalescence of socialism as a distinct alternative, labor unrest, and various revolutions across Europe, Pope Leo XIII penned his encyclical *Rerum Novarum* in 1891.[47] Addressing the condition of capital and labor most centrally, Leo articulated a number of themes

---

45 Leonardo Boff and Clodovis Boff, *Introducing Liberation Theology*, trans. Paul Burns (Maryknoll, NY: Orbis, 1987); Gustavo Gutiérrez, *A Theology of Liberation: History, Politics, and Salvation*, trans. Sister Caridad Inda, Rev. ed. (Maryknoll, NY: Orbis, 1988); Ignacio Ellacuría and Jon Sobrino, *Mysterium Liberationis: Fundamental Concepts of Liberation Theology* (Maryknoll, NY: Orbis, 1993); María Pilar Aquino, *Our Cry for Life: Feminist Theology from Latin America* (Maryknoll, NY: Orbis, 1993).

46 John T. Pawlikowski, "Modern Catholic Teaching on the Economy: An Analysis and Evaluation," in *Christianity and Capitalism: Perspectives on Religion, Liberalism and the Economy*, ed. Bruce Grelle and David A. Krueger (Chicago: Center for the Scientific Study of Religion, 1986); Charles E. Curran, "Catholic Social Teaching," *The Good Society* 10, no. 1 (2001); Edward DeBerri, James Hug, and Peter Henriot, *Catholic Social Teaching: Our Best Kept Secret*, 4th ed. (New York: Orbis, 2003); Andrew Yuengert, "Roman Catholic Economics," in *The Oxford Handbook of Christianity and Economics*, ed. Paul Oslington (New York: Oxford University Press, 2014).

47 For a helpful repository of encyclicals and other official ecclesial documents pertinent to CST, see the St. Mary's University Blume Library page: https://lib.stmarytx.edu/c.php?g=288002&p=1920734.

that would prove central to the Catholic church's stance on such issues in the coming century. Leo sought a middling position between the extremes of Enlightenment-based individualism and state forms of collectivism that squelched human freedoms. He critiqued the excesses and abuses of capitalist greed and worker exploitation, on one hand, as well as state socialisms that limited freedom and, perhaps most importantly, repressed the church.

This middling communitarianism, generally favorable to the market system while decrying its abuses, would remain in subsequent developments of CST. Other key themes in CST include an emphasis on human dignity as well as the dignity of work and the worker, in particular; championing the (nuclear) family as an essential site of production and reproduction, an institution that should be supported and protected; care for creation; social solidarity; and the preferential option for the poor, which, as noted above, would become central to liberation theology. While presented here in this part as a method of theology, CST is an ethical approach as well.

Anglican social thought is an example of a well-developed Protestant tradition of theological reflection on economic and political matters.[48] Anglican economic thinking had tended to favor the aristocracy, and it was typically the Methodists in England who had addressed the laborers and poor.[49] In the mid-nineteenth century, however, thinkers such as Frederick Maurice, Charles Kingsley, and John Ludlow sought to address Christianity's response to socialism and with it the church's responsibility toward the poor. A diverse body of thought that cannot here be summarized, Anglican social thought was generally critical of laissez-faire economics but also resistant to state socialism. It

48 Robert Worthington Smith, "Religious Influences in the Background of the British Labour Party," *The Southwestern Social Science Quarterly* 37, no. 4 (1957); Mark Bevir, "The Labour Church Movement, 1891–1902," *Journal of British Studies* 38, no. 2 (1999); Mark Bevir, *The Making of British Socialism* (Princeton, NJ: Princeton University Press, 2011); Kim Hawtrey, "Anglicanism," in *The Oxford Handbook of Christianity and Economics*, ed. Paul Oslington (New York: Oxford University Press, 2014); Marika Rose, "'It's Not the Money but the Love of Money That Is the Root of All Evil': Social Subjection, Machinic Enslavement and the Limits of Anglican Social Theology," *Religions* 7, no. 8 (2016); Stephen Spencer, *Theology Reforming Society: Revisiting Anglican Social Theology* (London: SCM Press, 2017); Luke Bretherton, "Anglican Political Theology," in *The Wiley Blackwell Companion to Political Theology*, ed. William T. Cavanaugh and Peter Scott (Hoboken, NJ: John Wiley & Sons, 2018); Michael Northcott, "Political Economy," in *The Wiley Blackwell Companion to Political Theology*, ed. William T. Cavanaugh and Peter Scott (Hoboken, NJ: John Wiley & Sons, 2018); Gary Dorrien, "Economic Democracy as Political Theology: The British Anglican Socialist Tradition," *Anglican Theological Review* 102, no. 4 (2020).

49 One classic study of Methodism's role in championing the poor but also in making them more docile and disciplined workers is E. P. Thompson, *The Making of the English Working Class* (New York: Pantheon, 1964).

insisted on the church's responsibility toward the poor and set forth the gospel critique of total privatization of property and harsh treatment of laborers. But it also rejected fully socialized and centrally regulated economies as advocated by forms of Marxism. Instead, many Anglican social thinkers advocated for "guild socialism," as a middling way that centered worker control over industry as opposed to oversight by state bureaucrats.

While always in dialogue, Anglicanism is distinct from various other Protestant traditions on the continent. We can find distinctive Lutheran and Calvinist approaches to economy, for instance, in addition to radical Reformation traditions, such as extensive Anabaptist engagement with economic concerns. These approaches draw on doctrinal distinctives of the traditions or retrieve the thought of founding figures in their respective movements.[50] One noteworthy site of contention concerns the responsibility of Calvinism for capitalist development, given Max Weber's influential thesis about the role of such communities in fueling the rise of capitalist enterprise. Contending against Weber's claims, some thinkers are concerned to exonerate Calvin from such associations or, in the least, heavily nuance interpretation by closer attention to Calvin's actual teaching.[51] Noteworthy as well are developments in colonial offshoots of these traditions, grappling with problematic legacies, such as Reformed thought in South Africa addressing apartheid as well as the racialization of labor dynamics and colonial extraction.[52]

---

50 Gerald Schlabach, *And Who is My Neighbor?: Poverty, Privilege, and the Gospel of Christ* (Scottdale, PA: Herald Press, 1990); Edward Dommen and James D. Bratt, eds., *John Calvin Rediscovered: The Impact of His Social and Economic Thought* (Louisville, KY: Westminster John Knox Press, 2007); David H. Eaton, "The Economists of the Reformation: An Overview of Reformation Teaching Concerning Work, Wealth, and Interest," *SAGE Open* 3, no. 3 (2013); Carter Lindberg and Paul Wee, *The Forgotten Luther: Reclaiming the Social-Economic Dimension of the Reformation* (Minneapolis: Lutheran University Press, 2016).

51 William J. Bouwsma, *John Calvin: A Sixteenth-Century Portrait* (New York: Oxford University Press, 1988); André Biéler, *Calvin's Economic and Social Thought*, trans. James Greig (Geneva: World Council of Churches, 2006); Matthias Freudenberg, "Economic and Social Ethics in the Work of John Calvin," *HTS: Theological Studies* 65, no. 1 (2009). For reevaluation of Weber's thesis, see, e.g., Philip S. Gorski, *The Protestant Ethic Revisited* (Philadelphia: Temple University Press, 2011).

52 For South Africa, see, e.g., John W. De Gruchy, *Liberating Reformed Theology: A South African Contribution to an Ecumenical Debate* (Grand Rapids, MI: Eerdmans, 1991); Nico Koopman, "Theology and the Fulfillment of Social and Economic Rights," in *Theories of Social and Economic Justice*, ed. A. van der Walt (Stellenbosch: Sunmedia, 2005); Rothney S. Tshaka, "On Being African and Reformed? Towards an African Reformed Theology Enthused by an Interlocution of Those on the Margins of Society," *HTS: Theological Studies* 70, no. 1 (2014). On Lutheranism in a global context that also addresses colonialism, see, e.g., Ulrich Duchrow, *Alternatives to Global Capitalism: Drawn from Biblical History, Designed*

From a broadly Protestant position, Kathryn Tanner's work has helped to define the field in terms of recent theological reflection on economy. Tanner approaches economic concerns from traditional systematic theology, informed by Anglican, Reformed, and feminist perspectives, relating core doctrine such as the Trinity and incarnation to models of the economy and to economic problems. Her *Economy of Grace* establishes a framework for thinking about the connections, linking points, and contrasts between divine and earthly economies.[53] She marshals reflections on God's noncompetitive relation to creation to establish principles for economic relations based in turn upon mutuality and noncompetition. Her more recent *Christianity and the New Spirit of Capitalism* reviews theological principles for conversion, justification, and sanctification in the life of the believer. These she sets into contrast with countervailing principles of debt that lay claim upon and attempt to shape human lives in late, finance capitalism.[54] The theologically informed framework for conversion enables a conceptual break with the past to which many remain chained by the bonds of debt.

Marion Grau's *Of Divine Economy* is another founding text in this field that bears mention as a distinctively constructive theological approach in a Protestant vein.[55] Grau draws on feminist, process, and postcolonial theory and theology to engage economic themes in Christian thought and bring them to bear on contemporary economic concerns. In particular, she rehabilitates the "trickster" trope, mobilized in feminist and postcolonial thought, to construct a Christology that challenges oppressive economic systems. She draws on patristic ransom theory, with narratives of divine deception of the devil in a salvific exchange, to set forth principles of subversive resistance for those living under the strictures of global capitalism today.

In terms of Christian life under global capitalism today, Pentecostalism is another example of a Protestant tradition that exhibits profound relations with economy, as well as a growing body of reflection on such links. A dominant

---

for Political Action (Heidelberg: International Books: Kairos Europa, 1995); Paul S. Chung, Ulrich Duchrow, and Craig L. Nessan, *Liberating Lutheran Theology: Freedom for Justice and Solidarity with Others in a Global Context* (Minneapolis, MN: Fortress Press, 2011).

53 Kathryn Tanner, *Economy of Grace* (Minneapolis: Fortress Press, 2005). The agenda introduced by Tanner in this work informs many of the methodological concerns of my present study. Tanner was my doctoral adviser and her work has understandably left a significant impact upon my own. A pathbreaking earlier intervention that also sets forth relations between trinitarian and earthly economies is M. Douglas Meeks, *God the Economist: The Doctrine of God and Political Economy* (Minneapolis: Fortress Press, 1989).

54 Kathryn Tanner, *Christianity and the New Spirit of Capitalism* (New Haven, CT: Yale University Press, 2019).

55 Marion Grau, *Of Divine Economy: Refinancing Redemption* (New York: T & T Clark International, 2004).

strand of scholarship focuses on Pentecostalism's proximity to capitalist practices, such as various churches' use of the latest marketing techniques and televisual savvy in their methods of proclamation.[56] Others have explored the symbiosis between Pentecostalism (and related charismatic movements) and prosperity teachings.[57] There is a resonance between certain Pentecostal emphases on manifesting the gifts of the Holy Spirit and prosperity calls to manifest health and wealth as marks of God's favor. Beyond this uncritical Pentecostal-capitalist collaboration, some Pentecostal thinkers are advancing more critical and reflective interventions on the relation as well as on the potential challenges such movements might pose to economy.[58] Here the disruptive and superabundant characteristics of Spirit are marshalled against the ossification and scarcity imposed by capitalism.

Public theology is another important subset of theological approaches that engages economy. Public theology straddles the bounds of theology and ethics by making policy and other pragmatic proposals in response to certain challenges in society, both locally and globally.[59] While different definitions exist, my take on public theology is that it represents an attempt to relate Christian thought to pressing issues of concern for a discrete public or set of interrelated publics.[60] It does so in a way so as the make a compelling case for the

56 Jean Comaroff and John Comaroff, "Millennial Capitalism: First Thoughts on a Second Coming," *Public Culture* 12, no. 2 (2000); Benjamin Kirby, "Pentecostalism, Economics, Capitalism: Putting the Protestant Ethic to Work," *Religion* 49, no. 4 (2019).

57 E.g., Simon Coleman, *The Globalisation of Charismatic Christianity: Spreading the Gospel of Prosperity* (Cambridge: Cambridge University Press, 2000); Naomi Haynes, "On the Potential and Problems of Pentecostal Exchange," *American Anthropologist* 115, no. 1 (2013); Rebecca C. Bartel, "Financializing the Soul: Christian Microfinance and Economic Missionization in Colombia," *Critical Research on Religion* 9, no. 1 (2020).

58 Nimi Wariboko, *The Pentecostal Principle: Ethical Methodology in New Spirit* (Grand Rapids, MI: Eerdmans, 2012); Nimi Wariboko, *Economics in Spirit and Truth: A Moral Philosophy of Finance* (New York: Palgrave Macmillan, 2014); Nimi Wariboko, *Split God: Pentecostalism and Critical Theory* (Albany: SUNY Press, 2018); Shane Clifton, "Pentecostal Approaches to Economics," in *The Oxford Handbook of Christianity and Economics*, ed. Paul Oslington (New York: Oxford University Press, 2014); Keri Day, "We Need a Pentecost," *The Christian Century*, May 3, 2018; D. F. Sebastian, "The Economy is a Spirit World: Spirit of Scarcity, Spirit of God," *Journal of the European Pentecostal Theological Association* 39, no. 1 (2019).

59 An oft-cited example of public theology engaging economics is Stackhouse et al., *God and Gobalization*.

60 Classic statements include Paul Tillich, *Theology of Culture* (New York: Oxford University Press, 1959); David Tracy, *The Analogical Imagination: Christian Theology and the Culture of Pluralism* (New York: Crossroad, 1981); Jürgen Moltmann, *God for a Secular Society: The Public Relevance of Theology* (London: SCM Press, 1999). More recent interventions include Chul Ho Youn, "The Points and Tasks of Public Theology," *International Journal of Public Theology* 11 (2017); Sebastian C. H. Kim, *Theology in the Public Sphere* (London: SCM Press, 2011).

solutions proffered, solutions informed in part by Christian reflection as well as by deep study of and dialogue with the context and challenge(s) in question. Less a mode of evangelism or attempt to make the "case for Christ" in the public sphere (which is always an abstraction that does not exist in space/time), public theology makes concrete and delimited proposals to aid a set public in addressing a specific challenge. The test of success of a public theological proposal is not whether the public addressed affirms the validity of theology or Christian tradition, but whether they accept as relevant and useful the proposal offered. Public theology addressing economy would thus involve the study of a particular economic challenge faced by a specific public, seeking to bring Christian thought on economy to bear in ways that are relevant.[61]

The preceding approaches I have outlined are ideal types: in practice they are often blurred, especially given the contemporary tendencies toward interdisciplinarity and disciplinary deconstruction in many quarters of the academy and in religious studies specifically. Hollis Phelps's recent contribution provides an interesting case in point: he offers a direct reading of the Gospels and the sayings of Jesus from a philosophical perspective, fashioning a vision that is not overtly theological but that takes scripture and theology seriously as valid sources on their own terms.[62] What one might take as a scriptural approach, as in a plain sense reading of the Bible and production of ethical norms, or a theological approach of exegeting doctrine from these texts, is complicated by a theoretically dense and sophisticated intervention from continental theory. I would place Phelps in the category of philosophical approaches; but his method also resists reducing Jesus to a "secular" philosophical thinker and avoids evacuating the theological content of Jesus's claims. Approaches such as Phelps's increasingly seek to resist ossified distinctions and forge new paradigms.

2 Approaching the Economy

The economy is a central and pressing object of analysis in relation to Christian thought. The need stems from the global experience of the economy today and the substantial bearing that economic ideas, decisions, and policies have

61 For a fuller exploration of my views on public theology as well as application to the concrete case of payday lending, see Devin Singh, "Economics," in *T&T Clark Handbook of Public Theology*, ed. Christoph Hübenthal and Christiane Alpers (New York: Bloomsbury, 2022).

62 Hollis Phelps, *Jesus and the Politics of Mammon*, Critical Theory & Biblical Studies (Eugene, OR: Cascade Books, 2019).

on nearly everyone. The ways people encounter economic issues, practices, and institutions vary, and these different positionalities become crucial as we assess the economy and its impact. Matters of class location, race, gender, culture, geography, and history influence one's encounter with economy and one's response to it. The economy is a primary and broadly held concern, whether by its masters or those under its boot. Even so-called economic dead zones, places in the world excluded from participation in global exchange and left at subsistence levels of poverty, are profoundly, if negatively, related to the economy.[63]

The rapprochement between Christian thought and economy presumes some relation between religious belief and doctrine, on one hand, and something called "the economy" and the discourse about it called economics. The model of the relation may be undertheorized or be a central object of consideration. It is quite often implicit. I contend that greater awareness and clarity about how this relationship can be construed are necessary to improve the types of analyses that emerge from the encounter.

The question of theology's relationship to economics can be located within a broader exploration of theology's relationship to the world, to culture, and to society.[64] This is a challenge because theological speech attempts to name the transcendent, unnamable, or unknowable – or what is deemed to stand outside such earthly spheres. While theology is of course located within the human realm and is always finite, human speech about the divine, methodological issues emerge about how to relate transcendence back to the created or immanent sphere. These issues emerge in particular with theological claims to special revelation, otherworldliness, or the infinite qualitative distinction between God and creation, which lead to questions about how then to imagine the God-creation relationship. Challenges also arise in relation to truth claims when such human speech is inevitably conditioned by finitude, perspectivalism, history, and sociocultural location.

The various categories of engagement outlined in the preceding part raise questions of methodology since they highlight various postures for analyzing the economy. They also signal the models that scholars have in mind, whether implicitly or explicitly, when exploring the relation between religion

---

63 See Ankie Hoogvelt, *Globalization and the Postcolonial World: The New Political Economy of Development*, 2nd ed. (Baltimore, MD: Johns Hopkins University Press, 2001).

64 Tillich, *Theology of Culture*; Kathryn Tanner, *Theories of Culture: A New Agenda for Theology* (Minneapolis, MN: Fortress Press, 1997); Delwin Brown, Sheila Greeve Davaney, and Kathryn Tanner, *Converging on Culture: Theologians in Dialogue with Cultural Analysis and Criticism* (New York: Oxford University Press, 2001); Tracy, *Analogical Imagination*; John Milbank, *Theology and Social Theory: Beyond Secular Reason*, 2nd ed. (Oxford: Blackwell, 2006).

and the economy. Some approaches present a simple and unmediated relationship between the realms of Christian thought and economy. They use Christian thought to analyze, expound, critique, and influence the economy or economic principles. Another approach uses economic principles to analyze the efficacy and manifestation of Christian beliefs and practices. Still other approaches present models of transcendent or immanent connection between the two realms, while others imagine a blurring or near total elision between them. Whatever position one has, a self-reflexive account of why one adopts a certain approach enriches the analysis. Even unmediated or direct approaches, which in my view are typically problematic, might be defended if a case can be made for such an unmediated interface between Christian thought and economy.

In what sense does theology speak back to economy, how does economy influence theology, and what is the basis for critique and challenge – in either direction? It is important to develop a model for this relationship from which to then offer proposals for intervention. If the relationship is undertheorized, then the basis for such intervention is attenuated. This cuts in both directions: historically, theologians have taken pains to maintain a theological space untainted by the world of economy and its "filthy lucre"; but this creates a hermetic seal that potentially undercuts theology's ability to speak back to a world from which it is purportedly totally separate, and sequesters the ability for the sacred to irrupt into the profane.[65] This is typically the desire of those who set forth notions of sacrality.

While one approach is to view these fields as separate and unrelated, the dichotomous view has been raised repeatedly in recent years when Pope Francis's ethical condemnation of unbridled capitalism was met with critiques that the pope should stick to theology and let economists make pronouncements about the economy.[66] Theology has its domain of expertise in mat-

---

65 The expression "filthy lucre" has a long history, appearing in William Tyndale's (1526) translation of Titus 1:11 to render the Greek terms *aiskhrós kérdos*. The King James Bible (1611) expanded this and used the term in 1 Timothy 3:3, 8; Titus 1:7, 11; and 1 Peter 5:2 for variations on these terms as well as for mentions of money and greed more generally. While now archaic, the term lives on in expressions such as "filthy rich" as well as in the idea of "laundering" money. One can also find a tradition, perhaps related to this association, linking money with excrement and defecation. See, e.g., Norman Oliver Brown, *Life Against Death: The Psychoanalytical Meaning of History* (London: Routledge, 1959). See the discussion in Nigel Dodd, *The Social Life of Money* (Princeton, NJ: Princeton University Press, 2014), 149–58.

66 Among a litany of examples, see Alejandro Chafuen, "Pope Francis: Admirable Goals but a Weak Understanding of a True Free Economy," *Forbes* October 6, 2020, https://www.forbes.com/sites/alejandrochafuen/2020/10/06/pope-francis-admirable-goals-but-weak-in-understanding-a-true-free-economy/#72309dcc3b42. The critique of Francis

ters of dogmatic belief about a divine being, and economics is the science of human patterns of evaluation, production, exchange, and consumption. Their respective fields have no real overlap, except insofar as theology has, over the centuries, attempted to make pronouncements about the morality of certain economic arrangements. It is noteworthy, in this case, that critics of the pope's interventions typically affirmed promarket ideologies that also rejected government intervention. This raises the possibility that such protest stemmed not from disciplinary distinctions but from resistance to any critiques of and efforts to reform the market. Separating theology and economics may serve particular interests and cannot be taken necessarily as an uninterrogated assumption that trades on the purported innocence of "objective" scientific fields of study. While there is a place for recognizing disciplinary expertise, the defensiveness and boundary maintenance that emerge in such exchanges signal deeper political concerns and rivalries.

Another way to position these fields is to view theology as a source of potential moral evaluation and critique of economics and specific types of economies. Here, a relationship is presumed, and it is one of primarily unidirectional impact and influence. To the degree that we can set theology and economics into conversation, the latter may be shaped and chastened by the former. This perspective appears at work in a large number of theological assessments of economics. Yet, typically, in such approaches no conceptual or hermeneutical basis for the exchange is set forth.

Approaches indebted to Marxist analysis might exemplify the reverse position: here, theology as a field is shaped and influenced by economics. More precisely, such approaches tend to hold that theology, as a form of ideology, is shaped by material economic relations more so than by the field of economics (which might also be taken as ideological, depending upon the views under analysis). In this case, the economy and economic modes of production, power interests, and class relations determine the shape of any given theological position.

Put most simply, the approach I take seeks to hold these two directions together by acknowledging the ongoing mutual influence and impact of theology and economy. Stefan Schwarzkopf provides a succinct definition of this "economic theology" in his recent introduction to the field:

> [Economic theology] is the study of the forms of interaction between theological imaginaries on the one hand, and economic thought and

is explored extensively in Paige Ruane, narrator, "Episode 13: Catholicism," *Oxide Radio*, podcast audio, June 24, 2017, http://www.oxideradio.org/episodes/2017/6/24/episode-13-religion.

> economic-managerial practices on the other, both past and present. It identifies explicit and implicit theologies inherent in economic concepts, institutions and practices as well as the role of economic terminology within theological thought, both past and present.[67]

Schwarzkopf's summation provides an excellent touchstone for envisioning the relation. Rather than reducing one pole to a derivation of the other, I prefer to acknowledge both and defer claims to origins.

Yet even this approach of holding both poles together can take different paths. One might examine the mutual influence by outlining forms of analogical relationship. Building upon a long tradition of analogical thinking in theology more broadly, one maintains the separation and integrity of each field, looking for similarities of form.[68] While theologians have tended to use analogy as a way to speak of theology's relationship to the divine, however, analogy must be applied differently to the relation between theology and economy. The basis for analogy between these two is not the same as the basis for analogy between the immanent sphere of human speech about God and the transcendent divine realm. The latter presumes an infinite qualitative distinction between the two that does not exist between theological and economic discourse. Theology and economic language are both human creations and cannot sustain claims to ontological difference between them.

Moving toward closer relation, theologian Ida Simonsson has recently advocated for looking for "isomorphisms" between Christian theology and economic discourse.[69] When considering the claims of theology and economics, this means that "two arguments with different content can have a similar or identical shape."[70] As she elaborates,

> The roundness of a soccer ball and the roundness of a drinking glass when seen from above are isomorphic to one another. If the ball were a theological argument about what is truly valuable in human life, and the glass was an economic argument about supply and demand in competitive markets, my focus would be on whether or not they share a structuring

67 Stefan Schwarzkopf, "An Introduction to Economic Theology," in *The Routledge Handbook of Economic Theology*, ed. Stefan Schwarzkopf (London: Routledge, 2020), 4.

68 Tracy, *Analogical Imagination*; Erich Przywara, *Analogia Entis: Metaphysics, Original Structure and Universal Rhythm*, trans. John Betz and David Bentley Hart (Grand Rapids, MI: Eerdmans, 2014).

69 Ida Simonsson, "The Order of Value: Christian Theology and the Market Economy" (PhD Dissertation, Acta Universitatis Upsaliensis, 2021).

70 Simonsson, "Order of Value," 21.

> form – the roundness. In this case, they might both be premised on an isomorphic anthropological assumption: rational freedom of choice. That does not mean that they fill this structure with the same anthropological content. When two things share an isomorphic aspect, roundness, it does not mean they necessarily share a full structural identity. The ball is a sphere – the glass is not. If one changed one's perspective, one might not even continue to see the likeness in shape.[71]

For Simonsson, looking for similarities of form can reveal possible genealogical relations between these fields. Analyzing the isomorphisms will help us better grasp the logic of each argument and understand potential lines of influence between them.

The approach for which I advocate supports this line of inquiry and recognizes the ongoing mutual shaping of these fields. Such influence includes interpenetration of terms, tropes, concepts, metaphors, and other conceptual images. At times the lines between each are blurred and it becomes difficult to determine where one field ends and another begins. Beyond isomorphisms of form, however, content too has been shared. This raises the possibility that when theology engages economics it may be uncovering theological notions that were already deeply embedded within economics. Likewise, the influence that economic ideas have at specific historical moments upon theology may gain entry through the already embedded economic concepts within theology.

In my own approach, I have advocated the idea of homology as a way to emphasize the links and connections between the economy and Christian thought. "Homology" as I use it indicates a relation of filial connection, mutual dependence, and shared or related lines of conceptual descent. Drawing from the use of biological metaphors to explore historical, textual, and literary relations, homology in this sense indicates that theological language and economic language have informed one another and that the presently addressed relation between the two is best understood in light of this foregoing and longstanding connection.

Beyond the linguistic realm, I claim that there is also a relationship between religious and economic institutions and practices. Homology signals the endurance of material relations and the lingering traces that show forth in metaphors and larger conceptual systems used within the two fields. Thus, exploring the relation between Christian thought and economic theory also necessitates paying attention to the relation between Christian practices and

71 Simonsson, "Order of Value," 21–22.

economic arrangements. "Homology" emphasizes conceptual links and transfers and as such transcends "analogy" as an effort to demarcate similarity across difference.[72]

The substantial amount of blurring between fields also raises the possibility that the proximity between theology and economy may point to a time when the fields were one. In other words, it is possible that theology and economics stem from a common discourse and are attempts either to describe the same phenomena in different language or different phenomena with the same language. As Schwarzkopf puts it,

> Economic theology pushes genealogical inquiry backwards into the historical space before the original distinction between theology and economics as separate disciplines. In other words, economic theologians of course read the contemporary world in terms of clashes between and co-adaptations of economics *and* theology. But they also ask to what extent we might understand economics *as* a form of theology.[73]

This blurring can be approached in at least two ways. On one hand, we might consider how theological and economic concepts represented a common set of discourses in the ancient and medieval worlds, stemming from a more unified worldview and frame of reference. Thus, the blurring speaks to a common heritage in general scholarly discourse, a discourse governed by theologically oriented concerns. Concerns about the economy were expressed in terms determined by a theological worldview. Of course, this view can be problematized when the actual and lived histories of diverse communities are included to disrupt this monolithic image of scholarship, let alone society. Distinct languages for and concerns about theology and economics can be traced back at least to the Greeks, to whom Western traditions owe many of our categorical distinctions that formed the basis of scientific inquiry. Even ancient Near Eastern civilizations that preceded the Greeks had discrete terms and rituals for practices we would describe as religious or economic. In other words, it is inaccurate to claim that the blurring of theology and economics is a pervasive premodern phenomenon and that their separation is only the result of modernity. While I and others emphasize the significance of the scientific distinction

72 Singh, *Divine Currency*, 17–22. See also the discussion by and my response to Sean Capener, "When is Analogy More than a Metaphor?," *Syndicate* (February 3, 2020), https://syndicate.network/symposia/theology/divine-currency/.

73 Schwarzkopf, "Introduction," 5.

of fields in modernity that results in pitting theology against economy, this does not mean that all distinction between them was absent in premodernity.

Given these difficulties, positing this past horizon of blurring can be taken, on the other hand, to invoke a prehistory, a time before the historical record and the emergence of writing. This move imagines moments where communal life and language were presumably less differentiated and where the ideas, practices, and institutions now marked as religion, politics, and economics were still of a piece. What this possibility suggests is that the things yearned for, grasped at, marked, allocated, and elevated in today's distinct fields may have been perceived as part of the same complex. Only as societies complexified and as the division of labor increased has greater specification and delineation progressed.

This approach is marked by difficulties, such as the rather blatant problem of accessing such prehistory, save by educated guesses through archaeology and comparative anthropology. Appeals to so-called premodern and primitive hunter-gatherer communities in existence today face the challenge that most such communities have emerged in conjunction with, even if in distinction from, complex civilizations, and may reflect such interactions.[74] Many communities have had historical contact with settlers, traders, and other colonizers for centuries. We also have no clear basis to claim that such contemporary "primitive" communities mirror what ancient societies looked like. The claim that what we take to be "simple" societies today are the archaic building blocks of modern, "complex" societies has been vigorously contested.[75] All of this means that this claim to a potential blurring, overlap, or even indistinction of religion and economy operates as an intuition that might direct our theorizing and influence the kinds of questions we ask and models we form, but can never be invoked authoritatively as evidence. Here it functions as a heuristic mechanism, holding out the hint of a radical proximity between these discourses, the connections for which must be demonstrated not by the endless quest for an originary moment, but through the conceptual analysis that lays bare the elision in whatever periods to which we have access. It also serves as a constant motivation to question rigid field demarcations and to remain attuned to porous boundaries with ongoing exchanges.

---

74 Marshall Sahlins, *How "Natives" Think: About Captain Cook, for Example* (Chicago: University of Chicago Press, 1995).

75 Tomoko Masuzawa, *In Search of Dreamtime: The Quest for the Origin of Religion* (Chicago: University of Chicago Press, 1993); Tomoko Masuzawa, *The Invention of World Religions, or, How European Universalism Was Preserved in the Language of Pluralism* (Chicago: University of Chicago Press, 2005).

2.1 *Modeling the Economy*

The central role played by the economy in the lived experience of most people is due in part to globalization, but also derives from a history of colonization. In other words, the broad impact exerted by a set of ideas and tactics around the economy has a concrete history of implementation, tied to the legacy of conquest and the search for resources and political power. Crucially, however, this broad dissemination and the widespread encounters with economy are also a result of the historical process of economic "disembedding," described by the economic historian Karl Polanyi. The capacity for Christian thought to address something called the "economy" and to enter into dialogue with the field of economics is therefore linked to the processes of disembedding as well as coloniality and globalization.

Polanyi famously traced the historical and conceptual construction of the market as an abstract and reified object in his *The Great Transformation*.[76] Polanyi claims that in ancient society the economy was "embedded" in broader social relations such that it was not an independently conceived object.[77] Economic transactions and relations took place in the framework of communal concerns for honor, status, position, and stability, for instance, and the profit motive was not supremely developed, let alone valorized. As Polanyi argued, there was no market *as such* in the ancient or medieval worlds. Of course, there were merchants, fairs, bazaars, and other sites of exchange. Furthermore, people engaging in economic activity were self-aware about what they were doing. This is not a claim about the blurring of religion and economy in these moments, as just explored above. The ideas and activities were differentiated. Yet economy was a thing one performed or exhibited. It did not subsist "out there." Furthermore, as Schwarzkopf recounts, it did not subsist even conceptually:

> Although traders and trade exchange existed in antiquity, "the" market actually did not exist as a concept in Greek thought. Although *agora* and *emporion* are often used as equivalents, both were directly identifiable *spaces*, not the invisible institutions and strategies of social relations that modern thinkers associate with the *concept* of market. When the term *agora* appeared in the sixth century BC in Greece, it referred to an open space in which people gathered *to hold* a market. Similarly, *emporion* was the term for a house, a trading station or a market town where trade was held by traders passing through (from *en* + *poros* = "to pass through"). Just

76 Karl Polanyi, *The Great Transformation* (New York: Rinehart, 1944).

77 Karl Polanyi, *Trade and Market in the Early Empires* (Glencoe, IL: Free Press, 1957).

as "the" economy did not exist in antiquity, the concept of the market is a much more recent invention, too.[78]

Of course, in modernity, despite a robust and highly reified conception of the market, the economy as such remains an abstraction. Where can one go to find "the economy" or "the market"? Yet they have been constituted as objects of reflection and, as such, as projections onto the social realm.

This creation of the economy was superintended by theorists resistant to political control or, more accurately, by those keen to direct political control toward ends that favored market movers in business and industry.[79] Early modern political economy and economic science as fields of inquiry arose as discourses for analyzing and managing – and, some would argue, fashioning – this market abstraction. One way to do this was to repress the market's human realities, particularly the various and inescapable idiosyncrasies of history and culture, let alone individual human proclivities. Such market reification is bound up with the logic of what has come to be called "market fundamentalism," where a simplistic and stripped-down version of market principles are elevated and enforced as dogma.[80] Despite its global character, existential preeminence, and psychic dominance, the market as an entity remains an abstraction that cannot be located in space and time.[81]

Creating an abstract, enclosed, disembedded conceptual entity known as a private yet (paradoxically) free market is also tied to the history of the enclosure movement and primitive accumulation. Enclosure refers to the process of land privatization that took place in Europe in the seventeenth and eighteenth centuries. Ecclesial and common lands were transferred by the state into the

78 Schwarzkopf, "Markets and Marketization," 167–8. Schwarzkopf notes that "economy" and "market" are not synonymous. This distinction is important although it is not one I explore here.

79 R. H. Tawney claims that early market theorists in England were predominantly those engaged in business and exchange as opposed to academic theorizing: "Economic science developed in England, not, as in Germany, as the handmaid of public administration, nor, as in France, through the speculations of philosophers and men of letters, but as the interpreter of the practical interests of the City. With the exception of Petty and Locke, its most eminent practitioners were businessmen, and the questions which excited them were those, neither of production nor of social organization, but of commerce and finance – the balance of trade, tariffs, interest, currency and credit." Tawney, *Religion and the Rise of Capitalism*, 126.

80 E.g., Fred L. Block and Margaret R. Somers, *The Power of Market Fundamentalism: Karl Polanyi's Critique* (Cambridge, MA: Harvard University Press, 2014).

81 Devin Singh, "Defaced Coins in a Utopian Market," *Political Theology Network Blog*, July 9, 2020, https://politicaltheology.com/defaced-coins-in-a-utopian-market/.

hands of private aristocrats who themselves were funding the state. In other words, in the early modern era, *state-backed* and *legal* processes were responsible for the construction of privatized land holdings, the commodification of labor power, and the intensification of private property rights. These centuries at the dawn of the newly constructed "free" market saw the decline of public and common lands in Europe, accessible to and useable by all, the erection of boundaries and walls to demarcate private property, the expulsion of serfs and peasantry from land access, and the creation of exploited wage laborers who could return to work the land at a loss to themselves and gain to their employer.[82]

This process is tied directly to primitive accumulation. Karl Marx invoked the term as he sought to explain where the initial surplus – or "deposit" of capital – came from to fund early capitalist enterprises and enable massive expansion of privatized production. The source, he claimed, came precisely from this violent seizure of land, as well as church assets. Internal conquest within Europe was the fuel to get the engines of capitalism moving, as primitive – or early – accumulation through force set further cycles of accumulation into motion.

What I have termed internal conquest in Europe in the form of land possession and asset seizure was interwoven with the genocidal pillage of native and enslaved peoples and of the earth and soil during colonization.[83] Internal and external conquests were of a piece. The *encomienda* and plantation were experiments in enclosure practiced in the context of extreme brutality and dehumanization. The unaccountable violence of such sites then allowed the importation of tempered techniques of oversight and control from the periphery to the center, to be used against peasants and later mill and factory workers during industrialization in Europe. Such sites of expropriation at the colonial periphery were of course in no way peripheral, and the development of the global economy as such is unthinkable without slavery as a primary engine of unremunerated value creation.[84] Thus primitive accumulation must also include the early seizure of land and labor power in the New World as sources of enrichment for European capitalist growth.

Furthermore, as Silvia Federici's important work has shown, European privatization, colonization, and the slave trade intersected with new layers of

82 Polanyi, *The Great Transformation*; Randal Joy Thompson, *Proleptic Leadership on the Commons: Ushering in a New Global Order* (Bingley, UK: Emerald, 2020).

83 Eduardo Galeano, *Open Veins of Latin America: Five Centuries of the Pillage of a Continent*, 25th anniversary ed. (New York: Monthly Review Press, 1997).

84 Edward E. Baptist, *The Half Has Never Been Told: Slavery and the Making of American Capitalism* (New York: Basic Books, 2014).

policing and control of women's bodies as sites of reproductive power.[85] The infamous witch hunts in late medieval Europe and the New World coincided with attempts to control, allocate, and reappropriate female bodies and labor in relation to an emerging mode of production: capitalism. The primitive accumulation that sequestered peasant labor and expropriated enslaved labor also required the labor of biological and social reproduction, which came to fall on women. Witches represented figures of rebellion, imagined or real, that resisted the ecclesial and state-mandated gender norms that posited women as domestic laborers to engage in affective care work, biological (re)production, and maintenance of the worker. The witch hunt for Federici is a marker of the religious, political, and economic upheaval of primitive accumulation and the ways it played out on gendered bodies.

Ironically, after violent and coercive intervention had constructed the market according to the interests of aristocratic, land-owning, and entrepreneurial classes, market theorists presented the economy as an independent, natural, and spontaneous sphere requiring neither regulation nor intervention. Early theorists of the market, most notably Adam Smith, presented it as an abstract entity, conceptually distinct from the social and political relationships in which exchange functions.[86] Thus, when we enter into discussions about engaging something called the modern economy or market system, we must also bear in mind its relatively recent historical creation, a process and history that, as Marx put it, "is written in the annals of [hu]mankind in letters of blood and fire."[87] We must further bear in mind that actual manifestations of the market are highly varied, involve layers of complex institutionalization, forms of infrastructure, and types of technology. In other words, when markets show up in the world, they are diverse and subject to materiality, history, and flux.

The modern conception of the market as a self-enclosed, self-governing entity is therefore a political and legal construction, and rhetoric of its spontaneous existence dissimulates such origins. Despite such attempts at conceptual juxtaposition, the "state and economy are not analytically autonomous realms but are mutually constituting spheres of activity," and "both states

85 Silvia Federici, *Caliban and the Witch: Women, the Body, and Primitive Accumulation* (Brooklyn, NY: Autonomedia, 2004).

86 Smith's theorizations of the market are described in Friedman, *Religion and the Rise of Capitalism*. I critique the ways that Friedman risks perpetuating abstract models of the market in his depiction of Smith, in Devin Singh, "Religion, Economics, and the Stories We Tell," *Harvard Divinity Bulletin* Autumn/Winter (2021), https://bulletin.hds.harvard.edu/religion-economics-and-the-stories-we-tell/.

87 Karl Marx, *Capital: A Critique of Political Economy*, trans. Ben Fowkes, vol. 1 (London: Penguin Books, 1976), 875.

and economies are embedded in societies that have specific institutional structures."[88] While political discourse purports to focus on the activities of persons and groups, economics, as the result of an intentional type of self-presentation, has been gradually abstracted and formally conceived, excising the human element.[89] Counterintuitively, human factors in exchange come to be seen as encumbrances to rational modeling and conceptualization, such that economists reduce their practice to formulas and algorithms, with quantitative and predictive applications. The nineteenth- and early-twentieth-century *Methodenstreit* or "conflict over methods" within social sciences contributed to the separation of political science from economic science and the further removal of economics from historical and sociological grounding.[90]

The modern economy remains linked to the political and social realms in significant ways and has never escaped enculturation.[91] Mark Granovetter's

88 Fred Block and Peter Evans, "The State and the Economy," in *The Handbook of Economic Sociology*, ed. Neil J. Smelser and Richard Swedberg (Princeton, NJ: Princeton University Press, 2005), 505.

89 Studies exploring this historical process include Hirschman, *The Passions and the Interests*; Don Patinkin and Otto Steiger, "In Search of the 'Veil of Money' and the 'Neutrality of Money': A Note on the Origin of Terms," *Scandinavian Journal of Economics* 91, no. 1 (1989).

90 Harald Hagemann, Yukihiro Ikeda, and Tamotsu Nishizawa, *Austrian Economics in Transition: From Carl Menger to Friedrich Hayek* (New York: Palgrave Macmillan, 2010); Kiichiro Yagi, *Austrian and German Economic Thought* (New York: Routledge, 2010); Keith Tribe, *Strategies of Economic Order: German Economic Discourse, 1750–1950* (Cambridge; New York: Cambridge University Press, 1995); Geoffrey K. Ingham, "On the Underdevelopment of the 'Sociology of Money'," *Acta Sociologica* 41, no. 1 (1998).

91 It is at times unclear whether Polanyi means to suggest that the modern market is actually disembedded or is made to appear so. Is there is an actual institutional break with ancient society or merely a conceptual shift? Granovetter and Swedberg charge Polanyi with inconsistency, noting that some ancient economies evinced disembedded profit motives, and that certain modern ones demonstrate embedded, social, and communal factors. See Mark S. Granovetter and Richard Swedberg, *The Sociology of Economic Life* (Boulder, CO: Westview Press, 1992), 10, 22n.1. I regard Polanyi as prone to rhetorical overstatement in the interests of a broader political critique of laissez-faire economics and what would be termed neoliberalism, and choose to read him charitably as retaining his anthropological convictions. He argued for the priority of a "substantivist" analysis of economy, one that recognized its historically situated and culturally embedded nature, over against "formalist" analyses that modeled economy on historically transcendent first principles. Substantivist analysis should be applied to the economy in all historical eras. To conclude that he regarded modern economy as truly disembedded obviates the force of his critique. What he laments is modern economy's *ideological construction* as disembedded, and he seeks to disclose its situatedness through substantivist methodology. Granovetter and Swedberg's critique reveals why it is the *abstraction* of the economy, not actual instantiations, that is the object of Polanyi's critique.

critical intervention adds nuance to Karl Polanyi's presentation of embedded economies, arguing that modern economies are "differently embedded."[92] This reconciles the apparent disembedding of the modern economy, as it is rhetorically and ideologically presented, with its actual embedding in social networks and institutions. Modern markets are conceptualized as distinct from societies, political processes, and cultural forces. This in turn persuades the modern mind to approach them differently. But such economies continue to reveal the importance of social relations and networks, as well as cultural and political factors that influence their formation and manifestation.

Such perpetual embedding nuances the rationalization thesis set forth by Max Weber, which laments the gradual disenchantment of the world through an ever-encroaching technicity and the quantification of reality.[93] Rather than straightforward linear and unidirectional development, as vulgar forms of modernization theory posit, society and economy are reoriented and reconfigured, and every historical context displays a variety of culturally conditioned economic forms. Polanyi notes that reciprocity, redistribution, and exchange, three primary economic relational patterns, can be glimpsed in a variety of historical eras and often coexist in one historical regime.[94] While an era may be characterized more by one mode, it is fallacious to exclude the possibility that the others are operative as well. To say that economy only develops one way, along one line marked in this case by capitalism, is sociologically and historically incorrect.[95] The specific social ties and communal dynamics that Polanyi identified continue to be intermeshed with the economy.

---

92 Mark S. Granovetter, "Economic Action and Social Structure: The Problem of Embeddedness," *American Journal of Sociology* 91 (November 1985).

93 This thesis is articulated throughout Weber's oeuvre. Centrally, see Weber, *The Protestant Ethic*. See also John P. McCormick, "Transcending Weber's Categories of Modernity? The Early Lukács and Schmitt on the Rationalization Thesis," *New German Critique* 75 (Autumn, 1998): 134–35.

94 Polanyi, *Trade and Market in the Early Empires*. Dipesh Chakrabarty makes similar claims both about the "vestiges" of prior economic forms remaining in capitalism and the incoherence of charges of anachronism in models of historical development. See Dipesh Chakrabarty, *Provincializing Europe: Postcolonial Thought and Historical Difference* (Princeton, NJ: Princeton University Press, 2000).

95 Even defining capitalist development monolithically is itself problematic, as studies in "comparative capitalisms" reveal. See, e.g., Peter A. Hall and David W. Soskice, *Varieties of Capitalism: The Institutional Foundations of Comparative Advantage* (New York: Oxford University Press, 2001); Glenn Morgan, "The Theory of Comparative Capitalisms and the Possibilities for Local Variation," *European Review* 15, no. 3 (2007).

2.2 *Theology in the Economy*

Just as the supposed disembedding of the economy in the modern period is contested and needs to be understood more properly as a different embedding and alternative economic positioning, so do narratives of disenchantment in relation to the economy need to be complexified. The dominant theory, partly resulting from Weber's reading but also due to a Marxian line of critique about the corrosive power of capitalism, has been that the growth of the modern market system corresponds to disenchantment, a stripping away of sacrality and the sacred, a decline of religion, and a removal of traditional notions of representation and signification that correspond to an enchanted world. The cash nexus and the price mechanism render all things exchangeable in a kind of brute materiality that reduces the depth of being to surfaces and strips the rich layers of human relations to flat, commodified interfaces.

While it is important to take seriously the concerns raised by such a narrative, grasping as it does at the profound upheaval brought by economic growth and the change in forms of social relations, to treat this as a linear process of decline of religion occludes as much as it enlightens. Even thinkers such as Marx, while claiming that capitalism denudes the world of what is sacred, used theological terms to describe capitalist processes, including the inordinate influence of the commodity form. Metaphysical subtleties, theological niceties, idolatry, and fetishism are key to his critique.[96] This signals the enduring relevance of theological frameworks in helping to make sense of the power and influence of the economy and the ways economic exchange, money, the price mechanism, and markets intersect with and influence the social and symbolic circuits that are often captured by religious terminology.

In other words, embracing disenchantment theory may rob us of an important set of tools to analyze and make sense of the influence of economy. Approaches such as economic theology remain essential for mapping the ways that theology operates explicitly or implicitly within economic discourse and practice, and how these concepts and practices in turn exert a "quasi-religious" influence upon individual and communal lives. It also opens the category to think of economics as a form of religion, as a "parasitic" religion, or as a derivation from more traditional religious practices, as various philosophers and social theorists have posited.[97]

96 Marx's theological metaphors are explored extensively in Enrique Dussel, *Las metáforas teológicas de Marx* (Estella: Editorial Verbo Divino, 1993).

97 Capitalism is described as the parasite of Christianity in Walter Benjamin, "Fragment 74: Capitalism as Religion," in *Religion as Critique: The Frankfurt School's Critique of Religion*, ed. Eduardo Mendieta (New York: Routledge, 2005).

Beyond the persistent politicization and enculturation of actual economic structures, it is possible to discern forms of "reenchantment." Religion and economy are often reconfigured together rather than separated in modernity.[98] This reminds us that religion, and Christian thought in particular within Europe, remained integral to the development of the economy and the market as concepts. From a genealogical perspective, one might consider how early theorists of capitalism appropriated and transformed prevailing theological paradigms of their day that proved useful in developing market ideas.[99]

Christian theology and forms of natural theology derived from it were much discussed objects of inquiry in the circles of the early economists. Indeed, the early modern, so-called classical economists, such as Adam Smith, were primarily moral philosophers interested in new theories of society, social order, and resource allocation.[100] As Schwarzkopf recalls, theologians also played a role in the Middle Ages in theorizing the rudiments of marketization and market mechanisms, four hundred years before Smith's famed reference to the "invisible hand" and his outlining of imperceptible and ungovernable market dynamics. Such theologians were speculating on the effects of supply and demand on prices and developing the rudiments of stock futures to hedge against losses, for instance.[101]

Yet early modernity witnessed a series of significant transitions and developments in questions of God's relationship to, management of, and intervention in the created world. There emerged a new focus on the purportedly rational structure of the universe, a universe governed by predictable and regularized laws, modeled on the rationality of God. Whether in deistic claims of an absent divine watchmaker, or Reformed theistic models of an inscrutable sovereign God who no longer intervened miraculously, the world was portrayed as clearly patterned, regimented, evacuated of mystery, and hence ultimately

---

98 See Eugene McCarraher, *The Enchantments of Mammon: How Capitalism Became the Religion of Modernity* (Cambridge, MA: The Belknap Press of Harvard University Press, 2019).

99 See, e.g., Friedman, *Religion and the Rise of Capitalism*; Charly Coleman, *The Spirit of French Capitalism: Economic Theology in the Age of Enlightenment* (Stanford: Stanford University Press, 2021).

100 See, e.g., Oslington, *Adam Smith as Theologian*; Oslington, *Political Economy*; Hill, "The Hidden Theology of Adam Smith," 1–29; Grewal, "Political Theology of Laissez-Faire," 417–433; Anthony M. C. Waterman, *Political Economy and Christian Theology Since the Enlightenment: Essays in Intellectual History* (New York: Palgrave Macmillan, 2004).

101 Schwarzkopf, "Markets and Marketization," 168.

observable, measurable, and predictable. These visions helped give rise to the modern natural sciences.[102]

Such paradigms also influenced the rise of economics as a discipline, which began as a subfield of Christian moral philosophy.[103] Early thinkers of political economy transferred ideas of the regularized and predictable patterns of nature – themselves derived from providence – into the sphere of the market. Centrally, these economists formalized a theory of *equilibrium*, depicting the market and its diverse and at times agonistic exchanges as somehow balancing out when seen from a high level – or God's eye view.[104] Various market transactions, however selfish and self-interested, would balance out to the net gain and common good of society.[105] Adam Smith's notion of the "invisible hand" arguably assumed an idea of a divine hand of providence. While he ignored or rejected explicit senses of an active creator orchestrating events, he shifted agency toward immanent market processes. The paradigm of providence informed and *may* continue to influence fundamental assumptions about market self-calibration and efficiency.[106]

While classical theorists were designing a providentially informed model of market efficiency, Christian doctrines of salvation also exerted influence. One dominant strand of soteriology claimed that a type of peace was established between God and creation, and among humans, based on a saving transaction that took place in the death and resurrection of Christ (John 14:27; Rom 5:1; Col 3:15–17).[107] We see hints of this impact of soteriological peace at work in the claims made by philosophers of the market who argued that commercial transactions were willed by God to bring peace and forge the bond of civil society.

---

102 Ian Hacking, *Scientific Revolutions* (Oxford: Oxford University Press, 1981); Michel Foucault, *Archaeology of Knowledge* (London: Routledge, 2002); Amos Funkenstein, *Theology and the Scientific Imagination from the Middle Ages to the Seventeenth Century* (Princeton, NJ: Princeton University Press, 1986).

103 Robert H. Nelson, *Economics as Religion: From Samuelson to Chicago and Beyond* (University Park, PA: Pennsylvania State University Press, 2001); Robert H. Nelson, *Reaching for Heaven on Earth: The Theological Meaning of Economics* (Savage, MD: Rowman & Littlefield, 1991); Anthony M. C. Waterman, *Revolution, Economics and Religion: Christian Political Economy, 1798–1833* (Cambridge: Cambridge University Press, 1991).

104 Bill Maurer, "Repressed Futures: Financial Derivatives' Theological Unconscious," *Economy and Society* 31, no. 1 (2002): 15–36; Jacob Viner, *The Role of Providence in the Social Order: An Essay in Intellectual History*, Jayne Lectures for 1966, American Philosophical Society (Princeton, NJ: Princeton University Press, 1972).

105 See, e.g., Bernard Mandeville, *The Fable of the Bees: Or, Private Vices and Public Benefits* (Oxford: Clarendon, 1924).

106 See, e.g., Hill, "Hidden Theology of Adam Smith."

107 Such peace is ritually celebrated in the "passing of the peace," which is a component of many forms of Christian liturgy that extends the peace established by the redemption of Christ as signified in the Eucharist.

Seventeenth-century business theorist, Jacques Savary, in his work, *The Perfect Merchant*, claimed that "[Divine Providence] has not willed for everything that is needed for life to be found in the same spot. It has dispersed its gifts so that men would trade together and so that the mutual need which they have to help one another would establish ties of friendship among them."[108] The view is glimpsed two centuries later in the American context, when the Episcopalian priest and economist John McVickar wrote: "For what other reason, do you suppose, has [God] given to different countries such different soils and climate and production, but that they should freely exchange with each other, and thus all be happier and more comfortable?"[109] We find furthermore the remarkable insistence that commercial transaction leads toward a lessening of aggressive impulses and a channeling of desires toward productive self-interest, such as John Maynard Keynes's claim that "Dangerous human proclivities can be canalized into comparatively harmless channels by the existence of opportunity for money-making and private wealth ... It is better that a man should tyrannize over his bank balance than over his fellow-citizens."[110] These perspectives reflect potential traces of a diffuse understanding of divinely willed peace accomplished by a redemptive exchange, that in turn is mirrored and applied by material exchanges among believers.

During an age of transition from Christendom to the new model of nation states, a transition marked in part by bloody and extended wars of religion, thinkers proffered the economy as a possible third way – distinct from religion and politics – that might ground peaceful coexistence. One conceptual foundation for these views, I suggest, was the doctrinal claim that peace could be based on a cosmic exchange, a transaction that liberated sinful humanity and enabled right relations with God and neighbor. The subtle merger of language of exchange and economy with notions of reconciliation in this early Christian doctrine led to the eventual fruition of such allegiances in explicit claims that economic exchange brings peace.[111] Language of self-discipline and individual ethics marshaled from the Christian tradition was also at work here. Becoming

108 Jacques Savary, *Le parfait négociant, ou Instruction générale de tout ce qui regarde le commerce* (Paris, 1675 [1713 edition], 1, as cited and translated in Hirschman, *The Passions and the Interests*, 59. Hirschman richly documents these dynamics across many thinkers and contexts throughout his text. See also Albert Hirschman, "Rival Interpretations of Market Society: Civilizing, Destructive, or Feeble?," *Journal of Economic Literature* 20 (1982): 1463–84.

109 Friedman, *Religion and the Rise of Capitalism*, 262.

110 John Maynard Keynes, *The General Theory of Employment, Interest, and Money* (New York: Harcourt, Brace, 1936), 374. Cited in Hirschman, *The Passions and the Interests*, 134.

111 Early Christian ideas of ransom are further explored in Singh, *Divine Currency*. On early modern attempts to reconcile self-love with neighbor love, see Grewal, "Political Theology of Laissez-Faire.".

a new person in Christ should lead one to a balanced, composed, calm, and rational self-comportment, manifested particularly in commercial exchange. Some Reformed theologians decried the passions and forms of spiritual or psychological "fanaticism," a refrain eventually taken up by secular theorists of the state and market. These manifestations of enthusiasm did not reflect of the "mind of Christ" or were not worthy of the postreligious rational individual, the "subject" of the Enlightenment.[112]

Thus, two key doctrinal areas appear operative in such transformations: providence – theologies of divine governance and management, and soteriology – theologies of salvation. Providence and salvation provided two theological scaffolds in a conceptual matrix that modeled a tendency for markets to calibrate and achieve equilibrium, as well as their capacity to enable peace and social stability. Weber's theory of the Protestant ethos attends to the surface level or practical manifestation of these doctrines. His account addresses the psychology and anxiety of believers grappling with the implications of providence and salvation. The question of predestination – which Weber claimed motivated Calvinist commercial activity to demonstrate one's elect status – hinges on belief in a sovereign God who plans and orchestrates history in particular ways (i.e., providence) and who makes central in such planning or decree a determination of who will be saved (i.e., soteriology). In this way, both providence and soteriology form twin nodes around which the nexus of theological ferment and market thinking might be examined. Arguably, themes of providential equilibrium and redemptive commerce remain present today, as pundits hail stable democracy and capitalism as handmaidens, and support market globalization as a route toward global political peace.[113]

2.3 *Engaging the Economy*

Modern Christian thought's engagement with economy calls for genealogical awareness. This need stems from the role theology has played in helping give birth to economic ideas and institutions that have come to dominate globally due to colonization and globalization. Theology's contribution to ideas of the economy and market provides one basis for theological engagements and

112 Hirschman, *The Passions and the Interests*; Jordana (Jordy) Rosenberg, *Critical Enthusiasm: Capital Accumulation and the Transformation of Religious Passion* (New York: Oxford University Press, 2011); Devin Singh, "Irrational Exuberance: Hope, Expectation, and Cool Market Logic," *Political Theology* 17, no. 2 (2016).

113 This is captured in Steve Forbes's oft-touted phrase, "Only capitalism can save us," or in Thomas Friedman's claim that no two countries with a McDonalds have gone to war with one another. See Thomas Friedman, *The Lexus and the Olive Tree* (New York: Anchor Books, 2000).

critiques of economy. This role includes the centuries of direct influence by the church during Christendom, the presence of missionaries alongside colonial administrators during the age of global conquest, and the continued implicit operation of theological assumptions and values in aspects of secular modernity. This means that Christian theorists should not naively imagine themselves communicating across a stark secular-sacred divide or position themselves as speaking from a pure ecclesial space. Christian thought speaks from a theological location influenced by various contexts, and it speaks to contexts already to some extent influenced by Christian theology and practices.

The complex history of development in economic attitudes, values, and institutions in the West is thus implicated in and through Christian history. The West has long been shaped by diverse forms of Christian preaching about the dangers of wealth, the responsibility toward the poor and vulnerable, the value of almsgiving, the evils of usury, the importance of work, the possibility that riches signal God's blessings, the virtues of capitalism or socialism, and the like. Such societies have also been affected, more indirectly, by Christian theologizing about God's redemptive payment through Christ, humanity's ransom from death, indulgences to remit sin debt, monastic vows of poverty, and other ecclesial practices that shaped societal ideas and opinions on economics even without direct ethical exhortation on such topics. To speak on economic issues from a Christian theological, ethical, or philosophical vantage point is to enter a complex space where many theological voices have long been at work.

In light of the history of disembedding that I have recounted, however, it bears asking if the break between economy and society is too far gone, whether economics is so reified and abstracted so as to have little relation to theology (and other humanistic disciplines, for that matter) despite this genealogy. Certainly, when economic claims are modeled mathematically, and social realities reduced to numbers, symbols, and algorithms, it is challenging to imagine a rapprochement. Orthodox economics has shielded itself from fruitful interaction by encasing itself in the guise of a hard science.[114] There is an intentional history behind this development, a succession of tactics by economists to present their subjective, social-scientific, and humanistic theorizing as a kind of law-bound physics in the interests of unassailable objectivity and cultural prestige. By becoming effectively wedded to state policy-making agendas and the government funding and authorizations that result, specifically in Anglo-American contexts, orthodox economics has garnered great success in establishing itself as "economics proper."

114 Julie A. Nelson, "Is Economics a Natural Science?," *Social Research* 71, no. 2 (2004).

Emerging alongside this form of abstract economics is a set of alternatives that are grouped loosely under the banner of heterodox economics.[115] This admittedly diverse set of approaches includes varying degrees of mathematical abstraction but also attention to history, culture, politics, and society as necessary for grasping economy.[116] Sociology and anthropology also have important subfields dedicated to the study of economy.[117] These fields assume economics to be a human, social, and historical set of ideas and practices and thus take such elements into account centrally. As such, they make excellent dialogue partners for theology, ethics, philosophy of religion, and other forms of socially attuned Christian thought that engage economy. Liberation theology has clearly blazed a trail in this regard by engaging in heterodox economic theories such as Marxist criticism, world systems analysis, and dependency theories. There is room for expansion, however, as theologians might take up a vast and diverse array of viewpoints and conversations among the social sciences.

More conceptually challenging for theologians at least, the impact of economic ideas and practices on theology also enables the rapprochement and dialogue between Christian thought and economics. For some, this link appears to undercut or invalidate theology's capacity to speak back to and ethically challenge economic arrangements, since theology is presumably "tainted" by the economy.[118] Some forms of theology have distanced them-

---

115 Frederic S. Lee, "Heterodox Economics," in *The New Palgrave Dictionary of Economics*, ed. Steven N. Durlauf and Lawrence E. Blume (New York: Palgrave Macmillan, 2008); Philip Arestis and Malcolm C. Sawyer, eds., *A Handbook of Alternative Monetary Economics* (Cheltenham, UK: Edward Elgar, 2006); John N. Smithin, ed., *What Is Money?* (London: Routledge, 2000).

116 Economist Charles Goodhart, who favors heterodox accounts, admits that "there is little doubt that the [orthodox] team has assembled the more illustrious collection of economists (plus the endorsement of Aristotle and Locke), and has expressed its analysis in more formal and elegant terms," while the heterodox "team has arrayed a more motley, fringe group of economists," and yet "has also received the support of a large number, probably a sizeable majority, of those in other disciplines, e.g., anthropologists, numismatists and historians concerned with the origin of money." See Charles Goodhart, "The Two Concepts of Money: Implications for the Analysis of Optimal Currency Areas," *European Journal of Political Economy* 14 (1998): 408–9.

117 Neil J. Smelser and Richard Swedberg, eds., *The Handbook of Economic Sociology* (Princeton, NJ: Princeton University Press, 2005); Richard Swedberg, *Principles of Economic Sociology* (Princeton, NJ: Princeton University Press, 2003); James G. Carrier, ed., *A Handbook of Economic Anthropology* (Cheltham, UK: Edward Elgar, 2004); C. M. Hann and Keith Hart, *Economic Anthropology* (Cambridge: Polity, 2011).

118 D. Stephen Long, "Can Christians Be Capitalists? D. Stephen Long Reviews Devin Singh," *Marginalia Review of Books*, February 15, 2019, https://marginalia.lareviewofbooks.org/can-christians-capitalists/.

selves rhetorically from economics as a facet of the fallen world. To be sure, there is rhetorical and ideological power in the construction of the sacred. Theology's self-presentation follows an age-old pattern of separation and distinction where "the holy" might be idealized and marshalled to generate social and political power. Theology presumably untainted from the world offers credibility to its claim to speak of things that are likewise separate from and untainted by the world.

Alternatively, this genealogy of theology and economy could show that a relation has long been established, a continuum along which theological economy and economic theology operate and elide. The types of influence and formation sought by theologians over economic ideas and practices could thus be viewed as part of that ongoing flux and relation. In the same way that it has become clear that much is to be gained by wresting theology from an exclusively skyward regard and revealing its feet on the ground in these categories of human identity, culture, and embodiment, there may be much to be gained by an open acknowledgement of theology's imbrication in economic matters. Just as it has come to be accepted that theologies emerge from particular communities and even reflect the politics of those communities, so they reflect and refract the economies of those contexts. While there has certainly been a rhetorical force and purchase achieved in denouncing economic injustice from the vantage point of theological ideas that appear far removed from economy, announced by voices in the wilderness proclaiming the direct "word of the Lord," a different kind of intervention and leverage may be possible from perspectives that acknowledge their economic interests and influences and emerge from the "mire" of earthly struggle.

Theology has tended to speak of itself as analogical in reference to the divine realm. Its language cannot hope to connect directly to or describe precisely what it grasps at in regard to the unknowable God. Yet, the relationship to economic discourse needs to be understood differently. While some may be tempted to remain in the realm of analogy in order to secure a pure space for theology in relation to economics, this does not follow. Theology as human discourse has a relationship to economics as human discourse that is different from theology's relation to the transcendent or divine. Theology's analogical relation to the transcendent is also different than economic discourse's relation to the empirical reality of the economy.

On one hand, the divine realm is distinct from the world (understood noncompetitively), and theology sets itself up with the impossible task of speaking of that which it, by definition, cannot speak. Economic discourse, on the other hand, speaks about things that are to some extent unknowable but for different reasons. We as individuals cannot think the totality of the economy or the full sum of production, exchanges, and consumption that generally fall under the category of the market. Yet the economy's epistemological status is different than the divine realm: it exceeds the capacity for human thought, not due to infinitude or an ontological distinction but due to scale and modes of perception. There are also important factors such as the internal psychological states of tens of thousands to millions of actors that cannot be ascertained. Economic discourse seeks to speak to that which is to a large extent unknowable, not because such data exceed or transcend creation but because they escape any single creaturely capacity for perception and comprehension.

Economic discourse has rarely if ever presented itself as apophatic, however, and such epistemological humility appears foreign in the territory of econometrics, algorithms, predictive statistical analysis, and the like. As noted, economists present their speech acts as a precise science, famously modeling themselves after early modern physicists, secure in the existence and accessibility of regular laws of nature.[119] Theoretical physicists have come a long way from early models of clear laws and mappable causalities, admitting to theoretical relativity and the perspectivalism that always inheres in any form of theorization. This shift toward epistemic humility has been slow to permeate, if at all, the realm of economic discourse. If anything, the internal and external pressures on economic science have edged it toward firmer claims of exactitude. With the new potential for massive amounts of data mining and predictive analytics, particularly when digitally mediated, economics touts shinier veneers of precision and certitude.

Somewhat counterintuitively, however, the limits on perception and knowledge do emerge in questions of governance and planning. A central tenet of neoclassical, laissez-faire, and neoliberal ideologies is the fundamental unknowability and hence ungovernability of the market as a totality. Thus, in contrast to the increasing confidence with which economists claim to model and predict market behavior, many market defenders maintain that such scientific exactitude does not translate into policymaking to regulate the market. Technocrats making external assessments do not have enough information about the market to try to manage it. Nevertheless, the market itself will convey accurate information internally to its participants to enable them to make individualized, utility-maximizing decisions. The result, such theorists claim, is immanent market self-governance that tends toward equilibrium. Epistemological claims about governance are tied to the politics of economists,

119 Adam Smith intentionally drew on the language and theories of Isaac Newton as he formulated his "laws" of economy and exchange. See Friedman, *Religion and the Rise of Capitalism*.

and reveal the ways attitudes toward market making are entrenched in philosophies of state and ideals of the kinds of societies that should be formed through the force of law.

Returning to theology's potential relationship to economics, while theology may need to present itself analogically with regard to the divine realm, it does not follow that theology's relationship to economics necessarily be analogical. Economic discourse, like theological discourse, is human discourse, grounded in history, society, and culture. The potential for these two expressions of grounded discourse to overlap follows from the reality that both emerge from the human realm, and by human agents who are typically divided only by academic training and disciplinary distinction. The latter, of course, can be significant, and terminological as well as major conceptual differences remain and often disrupt translation as well as productive dialogue. But the basic fact of interpenetration and mutual influence between these discourses, as forms of human meaning making and modes of academic inquiry, should be uncontroversial.

Since theology has been implicated in and bound up with economic realities, sometimes even playing a leading role in constructing those realities, it should operate from a position of consistent self-reflexivity and epistemic humility. Apophatic traditions have been good about remaining self-critical about theological claims about God, given divine difference and transcendence.[120] As noted, however, when applied to the social realm, such epistemic humility has a different basis. It is based in part on an acknowledged ignorance, that we are almost as lost about how the social world operates as we are about a supposed transcendent realm of the divine where theological predicates might align. It is also partly based on the acknowledgement that some if not many of the theological constructions and interventions offered over the centuries may have had unforeseen, negative consequences in the social world.

Furthermore, economic practice itself, that is, the world of exchange that economic discourse attempts to name, describe, and predict, is also part of the earthly realm and is an aspect of culture, history, and society. Because of this, it shapes theological production. Those who produce theology, whether professionally or confessionally, are human agents and actors who themselves live and move and have their being within a society deeply influenced by economic exchange, markets, and money. That such elements should influence and permeate the world of theology follows rather clearly.

120 For a recent important intervention on theological apophasis that has links to economic concerns, see Marika Rose, *A Theology of Failure: Žižek Against Christian Innocence* (New York: Fordham University Press, 2019).

Given this history of relation, questions then emerge about the usefulness of genealogy as a method of analysis and intervention. It is important to note that genealogy should not lead to determinism, despite our being accustomed to claims made by biological determinists that genetics equals destiny. This nondeterministic influence works in both directions: it is not self-evident that economics should take a particular shape despite its heritage in theologically laden worldviews, claims, and conceptual systems. Neither does it mean that theology is somehow "warped" or that it carries a genetic disease due to its relations with economy. Theology being informed by economic conceptions does not fix its horizon of possibility even if it has influenced its trajectories in actual history. Therefore I generally agree with critical responses to the use of genealogy that point out that a genealogical relation between theology and economy does not mean that theology is hopelessly tainted and forever silenced. As Hollis Phelps writes, "The use of economic language, metaphor, and conceptuality does not necessarily indicate an irretrievable entanglement with economic logic ... [since] economic language, metaphor, and conceptuality can be used against itself."[121] My nuance on this is that theology *is* irretrievably entangled with economic logic, but that this need not be a bad thing as such and also need not invalidate certain theological critiques of specific economic formations.

I have attempted to use genealogy to show the longstanding relationship between theology and economy as a way to complicate and refine theology's mode of critique. At the same time, the ongoing filial relations between these discourses enables theology to speak back to its relatives, its conceptual cousins, rather than to realms with which it supposedly has no relation. As Myles Werntz puts it succinctly, "One of the reasons theology is able to alter economic practice is precisely that it does not stand outside economic thinking."[122] Rather than the presumption that Christian thought challenges economic arrangements by virtue of its derivation from divine revelation (or the conceit of cultural supremacy due to Christendom), here the basis for confrontation comes from a kind of (troubling) solidarity with economic discourse. There is always space for reconfiguration and transformation. Economy as such need not be taken as evil any more than any other aspect of human society and culture. The mutual relation simply raises the more interesting challenge and promotes a more nuanced response of conceiving and describing transformation that occurs in, with, and under the elements of economy, including

121 Phelps, *Jesus and the Politics of Mammon*, 159.

122 Myles Werntz, "Review of *Divine Currency*," *Reading Religion*, July 9, 2018; https://readingreligion.org/books/divine-currency.

economic sin and brokenness, rather than described as a transformation that comes from without as a *deus ex machina* form of transcendent intervention and redemption.

3 Trajectories

This final part explores key themes and concerns developing in the engagement between Christian thought and economy. These may be sites of well-developed or nascent conversation. In light of the ongoing relations between these two fields, a variety of lines of inquiry are available, coupled with numerous modes of analysis and ethical adjudication. These trajectories are in no way exhaustive but are designed to indicate a range of what is possible and to encourage further delineation of sites of encounter and investigation.

3.1 *Political Theology and Economic Theology*

With the recognition that economics is not isolated from politics, as well as that markets are formed in conjunction with the activities of states, discussions of Christian thought and economy need to attend to the political. In this sense there is room for interaction with those engaging political theology, an admittedly broad and diverse field of scholarship. Definitions of political theology include at least three possible dimensions. Political theology may indicate theologies deliberately constructed to legitimate a political regime; political theology may critique such a sacralization of a particular political regime and advocate for an alternative theopolitical vision; or political theology may attempt to depict and mediate the relationship between theology and the political in terms of discourse, concepts, and practices.[123]

Similarly, economic theology may be a constructive task designed to support and shore up a particular set of economic principles and practices, whether in theologies of prosperity, theologies of the free market, or theologies of socialism, for instance; economic theology may be an attempt at critique of such a union, arguing for alternative theological economy that departs from or opposes any human economy; or economic theology may be the exploration

123 See, e.g., Annika (Yannik) Thiem, "Schmittian Shadows and Contemporary Theological-Political Constellations," *Social Research* 80, no. 1 (2013); Derek Simon, "The New Political Theology of Metz: Confronting Schmitt's Decisionist Political Theology of Exclusion," *Horizons* 30, no. 2 (2003); Michael Kirwan, *Political Theology: A New Introduction* (London: Darton Longman & Todd, 2008); Kieryn E. Wurts, "Neoliberalism and Political Theologies of the Post-Secular: Historical, Political, and Methodological Considerations in a 20th and 21st Century Discourse," *Religions* 12, no. 9 (2021).

of the mutual influence between economy and theology. A variety of conversations are emerging explicitly about economic theology in current scholarship despite economic theology arguably being a perennial theme in Christian thought. Yet, just as political theology has also been a consistent theme, but only has come recently into sharp focus, so economic theology invites direct reflection and further delineation.[124]

"Modern Monetary Theory" (MMT) is one of several interesting sites of engagement that highlights the nexus of the political and economic. MMT is a recent iteration of state and credit theories of money.[125] It derives from chartalism – the view that money functions as an authoritative symbol – and theories of fiat currency, which understand money to be instituted by sovereign decree, rather than as arising just from market exchange. As such, MMT links money to state power and to the role of taxation in creating the money economy. This theory rejects the idea of the spontaneous emergence of money within bartering economies as a means of exchange to overcome the so-called problem of the double coincidence of wants. This anemic "commodity theory" of money has been propounded since classical political economists first theorized the economy and assumed the function of money as a purely economic and immanent market technology.[126] MMT asserts rather that money is inconceivable without the role of state enforcement and coercion, as well as authoritative methods of representation and accounting. Considering money, debt, and other financial instruments and means of exchange with this model inevitably forces one to reckon with both economic and market

124 See, e.g., Patricia Owens, *Economy of Force: Counterinsurgency and the Historical Rise of the Social* (Cambridge: Cambridge University Press, 2015); Roberto Esposito, *Two: The Machine of Political Theology and the Place of Thought*, trans. Zakiya Hanafi (New York: Fordham University Press, 2015); Luke Bretherton, "'Love Your Enemies': Usury, Citizenship, and the Friend-Enemy Distinction," *Modern Theology* 27, no. 3 (2011); Luke Bretherton, *Christ and the Common Life: Political Theology and the Case for Democracy* (Grand Rapids, MI: Eerdmans, 2019).

125 L. Randall Wray, ed., *Credit and State Theories of Money: The Contributions of A. Mitchell Innes* (Northampton, MA: Edward Elgar, 2004); L. Randall Wray, *Modern Money Theory: A Primer on Macroeconomics for Sovereign Monetary Systems* (New York: Palgrave Macmillan, 2012); Arestis and Sawyer, *A Handbook of Alternative Monetary Economics*; Smithin, *What Is Money?*

126 While largely assumed by classical political economists such as Adam Smith, the commodity theory is set forth programmatically in Carl Menger, "On the Origin of Money," *The Economic Journal* 2, no. 6 (1892). For a thorough critique of the commodity or catallactic theory, see Geoffrey K. Ingham, *The Nature of Money* (Cambridge: Polity, 2004); Michael Hudson, "The Archaeology of Money: Debt versus Barter Theories of Money's Origins," in *Credit and State Theories of Money: The Contributions of A. Mitchell Innes*, ed. L. Randall Wray (Northampton, MA: Edward Elgar, 2004).

dynamics, on one hand, as well as the role of the state, legality, and coercion, on the other.

Theological analyses of money and debt are examples of routes into such conversations, given the ways that both money and debt interact with political categories such as sovereignty and law codes. Money can be understood in relation to a sovereign, governing center, as tokens and accounting mechanisms established authoritatively to oversee and regulate exchanges and to co-opt portions of such exchanges via taxation.[127] Debt instruments require the attestation of contracts as well as enforcement through legal statute, whether in the ancient world through recognizing debt slaves as a legal status, or through rights of forfeiture of property or other legally supported consequences of default in both ancient and modern times.[128] In the modern era, debt is so politically central that states set lending and borrowing rates with central banks, and all nation-states are funded in part through debt financing.[129]

Thus, theological critiques of money and debt should attend to the political dimensions that allow these socio-economic technologies to flourish. This means exploring the relation of the economic dynamics in question to ways theology supports political concepts and regimes. For example, the common political theological trope of God as reigning king, used to bolster forms of monarchical sovereignty, might be read in conjunction with images and tropes of God as overseeing a cosmic or redemptive economy, and thus in relation to governmental administration of markets and exchanges.

3.2 *Money and Debt*

As just noted, money and debt continue to be key sites of inquiry, particularly given that the modern economy appears increasingly dominated by matters of finance and the use of debt instruments.[130] While both technologies can be traced back for several millennia, there does appear to be an intensification and increased centrality of the two in the modern era. Historians of economy and of capitalism in particular note that capitalism thrives on its unique version of "capitalist credit money" that necessitates the fusion of public and

127 Georg Friedrich Knapp, *The State Theory of Money*, ed. H. M. Lucas and James Bonar, Abridged ed. (London: Macmillan, 1924).

128 Gregory Chirichigno, *Debt-Slavery in Israel and the Ancient Near East* (Sheffield, UK: JSOT Press, 1993); Alain Testart, "The Extent and Significance of Debt Slavery," *Revue française de sociologie* 43 (2002).

129 James MacDonald, *A Free Nation Deep in Debt: The Financial Roots of Democracy* (New York: Farrar, Straus and Giroux, 2003).

130 Luc Boltanski and Eve Chiapello, *The New Spirit of Capitalism*, Updated ed. (London: Verso, 2018).

private debts and the circulation of bills of exchange in a manner not seen before the rise of this mode of production.[131]

Money and debt are best thought of in relation, due to the ways that money functions as a token and sign of debt and presumes as well as demarcates debt relationships. Furthermore, debt appears to thrive under financialization and through accounting mechanisms as well as the proportions, measurements, and quantifying powers enabled through the concept of money.[132] In addition, the role that money plays as a conduit of sovereign power, exerting coercive force through the policing of forms of exchange that are licit and condoned by sovereign power as well as the centers of capital, brings new enforcement measures to debt. Debt instruments rely on contracts, oaths, or witnesses, various means of enforcement to require the return of the principal plus interest or other collateral and compensation. The circulation of money within sovereign fiat economies represents the debt of the sovereign disseminated among the populace, which bears the weight of the sovereign debt and yet still operates under the illusion that such monetary tokens can be equated with wealth.[133]

A variety of metaphysical, theological, and ethical issues present themselves for analysis. The increased financialization of all areas of life represents the further permeation of these instruments with new transformations in how money is perceived and how it shapes relationships and social life.[134] Reflections on the financial crisis and housing bubble have brought to light the role of derivatives and other debt instruments that demonstrate the gradual expansion of debt such that philosophers now speak of the indebted subject and the manner that debt structures the modern sense of self as well as the horizon of possibility for the modern subject and citizen.[135] Debt raises questions of

---

131 Geoffrey K. Ingham, *Capitalism* (Cambridge: Polity, 2008); Ingham, *The Nature of Money*.

132 A. Mitchell Innes, "What Is Money?," *The Banking Law Journal* (1913); A. Mitchell Innes, "The Credit Theory of Money," *The Banking Law Journal* (1914); Alexander Douglas, *The Philosophy of Debt* (London: Routledge, 2016).

133 Tero Auvinen, "At the Intersection of Sovereignty and Biopolitics: The Di-Polaric Spatializations of Money," *Foucault Studies* 9 (2010); Michel Aglietta, *Money: 5,000 Years of Debt and Power*, trans. David Broder (London: Verso, 2018).

134 Viviana A. Zelizer, *The Social Meaning of Money* (Princeton, NJ: Princeton University Press, 1997); Dodd, *The Social Life of Money*; Randy Martin, *Financialization of Daily Life* (Philadelphia: Temple University Press, 2002).

135 Maurizio Lazzarato, *The Making of the Indebted Man: An Essay on the Neoliberal Condition*, trans. Joshua David Jordan (Los Angeles: Semiotext(e), 2012); Maurizio Lazzarato, *Governing by Debt*, trans. Joshua David Jordan (Cambridge, MA: Semiotext(e); MIT Press, 2015); David Graeber, *Debt: The First 5,000 Years*, Updated and Expanded ed. (Brooklyn: Melville House, 2014).

inequality, economic injustice, and the erosion of social solidarity.[136] Money functioning as a sign invites theological analysis of questions of representation as well as analogy, homology, and metaphor.[137] While important work has been done on theology and debt, much more remains to be explored.[138]

3.3 *Neoliberalism*

While arguably we are nearing the end of the neoliberal moment that emerged in the 1970s, this does not mean that we have exhausted its analysis. Philosophical and theological assessments tend to be retrospective (and often postmortem). Thus, more work is required to make sense of the last fifty years under a set of ideologies, practices, and interlocking global institutions, both public and private, that have exacerbated economic inequality, dismantled

---

136 Richard Dienst, *The Bonds of Debt* (London: Verso, 2011); Miranda Joseph, *Debt to Society: Accounting for Life Under Capitalism* (Minneapolis: University of Minnesota Press, 2014); Annie McClanahan, *Dead Pledges: Debt, Crisis, and Twenty-First-Century Culture*, Post 45 (Stanford: Stanford University Press, 2017).

137 On money and metaphor see Marc Shell, *The Economy of Literature* (Baltimore: Johns Hopkins University Press, 1978); Marc Shell, *Money, Language, and Thought: Literary and Philosophical Economies from the Medieval to the Modern Era* (Berkeley: University of California Press, 1982); Jean-Joseph Goux, *The Coiners of Language* (Norman, OK: University of Oklahoma Press, 1994); Martha Woodmansee and Mark Osteen, eds., *The New Economic Criticism: Studies at the Intersection of Literature and Economics* (New York: Routledge, 1999).

138 E.g., Ahn, *Just Debt*; Luke Bretherton and Devin Singh, "The Axes of Debt: A Preface to Three Essays," *Journal of Religious Ethics* 46, no. 2 (2018); Sean Capener, "The Price of Charity: Christian Love and Financial Anxieties," *Journal of Religious Ethics* 46, no. 2 (2018); Sean Capener, "The Time That Belongs to God: The Christian Prohibition on Usury in the 12th–13th Centuries and the Making of the Subject of Debt" (Ph.D. Dissertation, University of Toronto, 2021); Goodchild, *Theology of Money*; Goodchild, *Credit and Faith*; Goodchild, *Economic Theology: Credit and Faith II*; Hollis Phelps, "Overcoming Redemption: Neoliberalism, Atonement, and the Logic of Debt," *Political Theology* 17, no. 3 (2016); Hollis Phelps, "Rethinking Debt: Theology, Indebted Subjects, and Student Loans," *Dialog: A Journal of Theology* 55, no. 1 (2016); Erin Runions, "Immobile Theologies, Carceral Affects: Interest and Debt in Faith-Based Prison Programs," in *Religion, Emotion, Sensation: Affect Theories and Theologies*, ed. Karen Bray and Stephen D. Moore (New York: Fordham University Press, 2019); Erin Runions, "Carceral Sacrificonomics in the Time of Pandemic," *Critical Research on Religion* 9, no. 1 (2021); Devin Singh, "Debt Cancellation as Sovereign Crisis Management," *Cosmologics*, Jan 18, 2016; Devin Singh, "Sovereign Debt," *Journal of Religious Ethics* 46, no. 2 (2018); Elettra Stimilli, *The Debt of the Living: Ascesis and Capitalism* (Albany, NY: SUNY Press, 2017); Elettra Stimilli, *Debt and Guilt: A Political Philosophy* (London: Bloomsbury Academic, 2019); Tanner, *Economy of Grace*; Tanner, *Christianity and the New Spirit of Capitalism*; Linn Marie Tonstad, "Debt Time is Straight Time," *Political Theology* 17, no. 5 (2016); Wariboko, *God and Money*; Wariboko, *Economics in Spirit and Truth*.

government safety nets, eroded the rule of law, and torpedoed any lingering philosophical vision for a common good.

There are competing theories about what defines neoliberalism. Common themes include the use of government, paradoxically, to enforce ideologies of less governance and deregulation. State control and oversight are extended concomitantly with monetization and financialization, such that audit cultures, forms of accounting, and the price mechanism are used as the primary and sometimes the only metrics for governmental administration and efficacy. Neoliberalism propounds ideologies of bootstrap individualism; entrepreneurship; individual utility; self-interest and consumer preference; and the privatization and corporatization of formerly public and common goods.[139]

Ethical and theological interventions have focused on the erosion of trust and of a sense of society and solidarity, the lost role of welfare and care work to tend to the vulnerable and marginalized, as well as a truncated anthropology that views humans as isolated, utility-maximizing consumers. Paradoxically, neoliberalism is a globalist movement that has relied on American exceptionalism, at times trading on American supremacy and enforcement of its principles, while at other times supporting capital flight and labor migration in ways that transcend – and potentially undermine – national interests and boundaries. Arguably it is the corporation that serves as the driver and center of agency for neoliberal agendas, even as corporate interests through lobbyists as well as CEO appointees to presidential advisory councils inform executive decision-making and legislation from the halls of government.

Neoliberal ideology is well beyond illusions of a free and spontaneous market, using state coercion to deregulate and create space for private owners and corporate interests to exert control. Neoliberalism has also gutted antitrust legislation and so enabled the formation of corporate monopolies that appear anticompetitive, dangerous for consumers, and against classical liberal economic principles. It has shaped business philosophy and corporate prioritization of profits and shareholder value over long-term and social goods. It has contributed to the erosion of public sector support, fueling mantra-like repetition of enterprise-based solutions for all problems faced by society.

A variety of theological themes within neoliberalism present themselves for analysis. Adam Kotsko has examined the practice of demonization of

139 Wendy Brown, *Undoing the Demos: Neoliberalism's Stealth Revolution* (New York: Zone Books, 2015); Melinda Cooper, *Family Values: Between Neoliberalism and the New Social Conservatism* (New York: Zone Books, 2017); Martijn Konings, *Capital and Time: For a New Critique of Neoliberal Reason* (Stanford: Stanford University Press, 2018).

vulnerable populations to reinforce neoliberal agendas.[140] Drawing on his work on the history of Satan, Kotsko describes the positioning of certain figures, such as the "Black welfare queen," as emblematic of the social evils that neoliberalism seeks to rectify and from which it promises to protect a white majority population. Despite the reality that neoliberal agendas work against the interests of the majority and particularly the white working class, such groups often support neoliberal platforms due to the demonization of others with whom they might otherwise be in solidarity.

Dotan Leshem has examined what he claims are the origins of neoliberalism in early trinitarian debates and models of pastoral practice in the Christian church in Late Antiquity.[141] Certain allocations of power and certain forms of administration, as well as notions of growth and consumption, have potential analogues in early theological concerns that may be carried forward into modernity. Certainly, as others have argued, neoliberal thinkers like Friedrich Hayek and Milton Friedman appear to draw on theological tropes and assumptions, even if advancing an ostensibly secular platform.[142]

The possibilities of the theological traces informing neoliberalism are amplified when one considers the nearly unanimous support that American evangelicals have offered to neoliberal pundits and ideologies. This elective affinity between evangelicalism and neoliberalism, explored for instance by William Connolly, raises the question of theological resonance and potential overlap between a theological worldview and the values espoused by neoliberalism.[143] Joshua Ramey has also highlighted the correspondences between neoliberal logic and a kind of divinization, addressing contingency and chance with an alchemy of predictive models and attempts at stasis to project a confident future vision.[144] Roger Green has located neoliberalism as an expression of the "eurochristian" colonial legacy.[145] Continued work is necessary both to understand the theological origins of neoliberalism as well as to consider ethical and theological responses.

---

140 Kotsko, *Neoliberalism's Demons*; Adam Kotsko, *The Prince of This World* (Stanford: Stanford University Press, 2016).

141 Dotan Leshem, *The Origins of Neoliberalism: Modeling the Economy from Jesus to Foucault* (New York: Columbia University Press, 2016).

142 Tim Christiaens, "Hayek's Vicarious Secularization of Providential Theology," *Philosophy & Social Criticism* 45, no. 1 (2019); Scott A. Kirkland, "Hayekian Neoliberalism as Negative Political Theology," *Political Theology* 21, no. 7 (2020).

143 William E. Connolly, *Capitalism and Christianity, American Style* (Durham, NC: Duke University Press, 2008).

144 Ramey, *Politics of Divination*.

145 Roger K. Green, "Neoliberalism and Eurochristianity," *Religions* 12, no. 9 (2021).

3.4 *Class, Labor, and Inequality*

Liberation theology paved the way for a critical focus on class within modern Christian thought, a site of analysis that remains essential.[146] As liberationist thought has diversified and increased in contextual specificity, class analysis has continued in conjunction with other intersectional factors of identity, culture, and politics. It has increasingly become recognized that class must be analyzed in terms of categories such as race, gender, sexuality, and ability. Debates continue about which of these to prioritize.

Closely related to class is the question of labor. Joerg Rieger argues, "The fundamental problem today is not distribution, or the lack thereof, but production and how we value it. Unfortunately, many contemporary theological critiques of the economy continue to overlook precisely this point and move directly to a critique of financial capitalism or the monetary economy without considering work and labour."[147] While debates can continue about which matters to prioritize in analysis, unquestionably the condition and fate of labor are factors to which we must attend. One can engage labor history and theories of organizing, as well as theologies and philosophies of work.[148]

There has also been an increased focus on matters of economic inequality and the widening global wealth gap. This is partly due to the rapid upturn in stratification between the rich and poor in the last fifty years. Neoliberal economic agendas and trickle-down economic policies have exacerbated rather than ameliorated such disparities. Liberation theology represents a long tradition that critiqued economic and political regimes that allowed a wealthy minority to control the lives and economic prospects of the poor majority. Further work on inequality continues to emerge within Christian thought, much of which interacts with recent economic research such as landmark studies by Thomas Piketty and Angus Deaton.[149]

---

146 See, e.g., Joerg Rieger, ed., *Religion, Theology, and Class: Fresh Engagements After Long Silence* (New York: Palgrave Macmillan, 2013); Joerg Rieger, *Opting for the Margins: Postmodernity and Liberation in Christian Theology* (New York: Oxford University Press, 2003); Jin Young Choi and Joerg Rieger, eds., *Faith, Class, and Labor: Intersectional Approaches in a Global Context* (Eugene, OR: Pickwick, 2020).

147 Joerg Rieger, "Rethinking Religion, Theology, and What Really Matters: The Ultimate Concerns of Essential Work," *Stellenbosch Theological Journal* 7 (2021): 4. For Rieger's interventions on labor, see, e.g., Rieger, *No Rising Tide*.

148 Luke Bretherton's work is a notable example of drawing on theories of organizing in conversation with Christian ethics. See Luke Bretherton, *Resurrecting Democracy: Faith, Citizenship, and the Politics of a Common Life* (New York: Cambridge University Press, 2015).

149 Angus Deaton, *The Great Escape: Health, Wealth, and the Origins of Inequality* (Princeton, NJ: Princeton University Press, 2013); Thomas Piketty, *Capital in the Twenty-First Century*,

Elizabeth Hinson Hasty's work engages the problem of wealth, challenging the focus on poverty as a problem and flipping the terms of debate to address the sin of excess.[150] In addition, the Skidelskys offer an examination of curbed consumption and proportionate living along Thomistic lines.[151] More recently, Mary Hirschfeld has written on Thomas Aquinas's views of the market.[152] This Thomistic tradition attempts to address the question of economic disparity through drawing on Aristotelian notions of proportionality and balanced living within the limits of necessity and legitimate desire. Another angle considers popular social movements as protests against inequality, such as those related to the Occupy movement and other forms of community organizing.[153]

More work remains to be done to understand the sources and solutions to inequality.[154] The problem of debt in society also exacerbates this issue, since debt is typically a way to try to address or exploit inequalities. Debt relationships only become possible in the context of inequality; and yet rather than closing the gap through ameliorative lending, forms of predatory lending instead exacerbate inequity through extractive terms that further impoverish needy borrowers. Further investigation is needed to reflect on issues such as payday lending and microcredit as well as theologically informed and communally based responses.[155]

3.5 *Precarity and Vulnerability*

Precarius originally meant "obtaining by prayer or pleading," stemming from the Latin, *precari*, to pray. Precariousness or the condition of precarity signal

---

trans. Arthur Goldhammer (Cambridge, MA: The Belknap Press of Harvard University Press, 2014); Thomas Piketty, *Capital and Ideology*, trans. Arthur Goldhammer (Cambridge, MA: The Belknap Press of Harvard University Press, 2020); Anne Case and Angus Deaton, *Deaths of Despair and the Future of Capitalism* (Princeton: Princeton University Press, 2020).

150 Elizabeth L. Hinson-Hasty, *The Problem of Wealth: A Christian Response to a Culture of Affluence* (Maryknoll: Orbis, 2017); see also David M. Cloutier, *The Vice of Luxury: Economic Excess in a Consumer Age* (Washington, DC: Georgetown University Press, 2015).

151 Robert Skidelsky and Edward Skidelsky, *How Much Is Enough? Money and the Good Life* (New York: Other Press, 2012).

152 Hirschfeld, *Aquinas and the Market*.

153 Joerg Rieger and Kwok Pui-Lan, *Occupy Religion: Theology of the Multitude* (Lanham, MD: Rowman & Littlefield, 2012); Bretherton, *Resurrecting Democracy*; Bretherton, *Christ and the Common Life*.

154 See the special issue on inequality and Christian ethics: "Focus on Inequality," *Journal of Religious Ethics* 47, no. 2 (2019): 217–354.

155 One study that addresses microcredit is Ahn, *Just Debt*. On payday lending see Singh, "Economics."

a state of fragility and dependence. The term's archaic links to prayer and petition invoke a state of radical vulnerability and need, such that only a god would hear and deign to help. Precarity invokes circumstances so fragile and desperate that all one has left is a prayer or supplication.

Precarity has so come to characterize life under modern political economy that social theorists have identified – or at least labeled – a new social class: the precariat.[156] Echoing Marx's proletariat, the precariat class label signals not only wage labor but the unpredictability of access to work itself, and hence to the monetary wages that circulate as the lifeblood of the present system. The precariat displays a radical vulnerability that comes when even the meager buffer of access to basic wages cannot be counted upon.

As casual, contingent, and disposable labor, the precariat is not merely vulnerable to the shocks in the system – rather, the system itself is the shock; for it creates and sustains the vulnerability of the precariat. Precarious existence is the norm.[157] Precarity's etymology invokes the state of hanging on a wing and a prayer, when a plea is all that one has left. The link to prayer is useful because it raises the question of how theological and religious factors might be related to constructions of precarity. It moves us to consider what theological traces linger in the production of vulnerable communities.

Capitalism's own precariousness causes it to constantly seek ways to deflect its own vulnerability, and the production of pools of low-wage labor and slave labor are two ways capitalism grasps hold on its unstable legs, causing mass suffering in the process. Forged over centuries through violence, conquest, and legal enforcement, capitalism is profoundly tenuous, making ideologies of its inevitability and naturalness all the more absurd. Capitalism's need for low-wage or even nonwage labor means that, as the system perpetuates, it will continue to produce communities that are vulnerable and that depend upon it, giving their labor for exploitative wages in order to survive.

At its inception, capitalism took root by creating precarity through the violence of primitive accumulation, as explored in the previous part. Since the generation of capital requires capital, the question arises of where the initial capital came from that fueled the rise of industry in early modern markets. The founding myth provided by classical political economists claims that, initially, there were those naturally given to industry and commerce, and those given to

156 Guy Standing, *The Precariat: The New Dangerous Class*, Rev. ed. (London: Bloomsbury Academic, 2016); Noam Chomsky, "Plutonomy and the Precariat: On the History of the U.S. Economy in Decline," *The Huffington Post*, May 8, 2012.

157 William E. Connolly, *The Fragility of Things: Self-Organizing Processes, Neoliberal Fantasies, and Democratic Activism* (Durham, NC: Duke University Press, 2013).

sloth and lack of ingenuity. The former instinctively added value to the world and also created opportunity and incentive for the latter. If the latter had no creativity, the tale goes, they could at least be motivated to work, offering the only commodity they had, their labor power. It is notable that Christian visions of noble and redemptive suffering were marshalled to undergird systems that exposed wage laborers to precarity. The argument was that such hardship would build their character, forged in a crucible of hard labor.[158]

As noted in the above exploration of economy, in reality primitive accumulation relied on the enclosure movement: the removal of peasants from common lands, the privatizing of public land through enclosure, possession of church and public land and goods by states and new corporate actors, and changing access to land and the materials of production – now mediated through wage labor. Founding acts by the agents of capital included the manufacture of precarity, as serfs were tossed off feudal and ecclesial lands, and only permitted to return as laborers seeking a day's wage. This is not to pretend that preceding serfdom was an idyllic state. Certainly, the feudal mode of production exhibited its own forms of precariousness and the creation of vulnerable communities. Yet capitalism radicalized these conditions and created new permutations of precarity.[159]

Slavery and the Atlantic system functioned in tandem with the enclosure movement as early drivers of capitalism. Much capital acquired in the phase of primitive accumulation, which enabled the funding of industry and new entrepreneurial expansion, was provided through unpaid, coerced labor. While the European expelled serfs were still recognized as part of the social fabric (if precariously so), and included in economic circuits via the wage relationship, the imposed slavery on native and African peoples, with no recompense or wage recognition, underscored their total exclusion and full precarity. They subsisted as barely within the system, as existing on its borders in a way that came to define its limits and its growth edge, underlying its expanding foundations.

Slaves as the limit case of precarity prove to be capitalism's grounding possibility. This is why, as C. L. R. James notes in *The Black Jacobins*, the slave was the counterpoint and complement to the new European proletariat.[160] Plantations were being established via the Atlantic triangle, even as enclosures were

158 Such nefarious theologies of "improvement" through impoverishment and exploited labor are well documented in McCarraher, *Enchantments of Mammon*.

159 For a review of this history, see McCarraher, *Enchantments of Mammon*; Federici, *Caliban and the Witch*; Thompson, *Proleptic Leadership on the Commons*; Pierre Dardot and Christian Laval, *Common: On Revolution in the 21st Century* (London: Bloomsbury, 2019).

160 C. L. R. James, *The Black Jacobins: Toussaint l'Ouverture and the San Domingo Revolution*, 2nd ed. (New York: Vintage Books, 1963). See also Nancy Fraser, "Expropriation and

taking place and land was being privatized in Europe. Both must be thought of together in the history of capitalism and modernity, and both remain as simultaneous objects of inquiry for Christian thought. Questions remain about how Christian thought contributed to the formation of proletarian and enslaved classes, how it conveyed and intensified vulnerability and precarity, and how it provides responses and interventions to address such concerns.

3.6 *Racial Capitalism*

The status of the slave as the condition of possibility for capitalism leads to a consideration of racial capitalism itself. Racial capitalism marks a variety of ways to think about the intersections of race, racism, and political economy.[161] It draws upon discussions of antiblackness, white supremacy, and the legacy of slavery in the West. At a minimum, racial capitalism marks the indelible link between racism and the operations of capitalism. From a simple historical perspective, the rise and success of capitalism cannot be understood apart from the extensive surplus value extracted from the unremunerated labor of Indigenous populations and of black chattel slaves taken from Africa. It is simply incorrect to extol the capacity for capitalism to generate wealth without including the central engine that enabled such wealth generation: unpaid, coerced labor. Thus, in addition to the dynamic of exploitation, which Marx and others highlight as central to capitalism, and which describes the extraction of surplus value from paid proletariat wage workers, expropriated labor, labor that is forced through torture and pain and that is not compensated, provided the backbone for capitalist wealth generation.

Torture was a primary means of labor extraction. Entrepreneurs and slaveholders collaborated to create ever more efficient and brutal techniques of confinement, humiliation, and pain, to extract greater levels of labor from enslaved peoples.[162] The experiments with violence and coercion in the New World on *encomiendas* and plantations represented the cutting edge of capitalist innovation. Removed from any ethical strictures about human decency, slaveholders and colonists would develop new methods for surveillance and

---

Exploitation in Racialized Capitalism: A Reply to Michael Dawson," *Critical Historical Studies* 3, no. 1 (Spring 2016).

161 See Eric Eustace Williams, *Capitalism and Slavery* (Chapel Hill, NC: University of North Carolina Press, 1944); Nancy Leong, "Racial Capitalism," *Harvard Law Review* 126, no. 8 (2013); James, *Black Jacobins*; Cedric Robinson, *Black Marxism: The Making of the Black Radical Tradition* (Chapel Hill, NC: University of North Carolina Press, 2000).

162 William David Hart, "Constellations: Capitalism, Antiblackness, Afro-Pessimism, and Black Optimism," *American Journal of Theology & Philosophy* 39, no. 1 (2018): 10. Hart is reviewing Baptist, *Half Has Never Been Told*.

labor coercion. These in turn could be modified and adapted for white workers. "Enslaved black people were the guinea pigs for techniques of labor extraction that would eventually migrate to the non-enslaved sectors of the American economy."[163] Before being implemented in industrial capitalism, practices such as time discipline, labor and production quotas, and leisure restrictions on the factory floor, policed under the watchful eye of the foreman, were tested in cotton and sugar cane fields under the boot and whip of the master.

In his poignant history of slavery as constitutive of capitalism, Edward Baptist cites a new mechanism of exchange known as the "faith bond."[164] This financial instrument presages the securitization and derivatives market in later finance capitalism. Reflecting on Baptist's work here, William Hart notes that "the enslaved were transformed from commodities into derivatives. More accurately, the value of the enslaved as asset-backed securities (derivatives) exceeded their underlying value as a commodity."[165] Essentially, slaves could be mortgaged if an enslaver needed to borrow against them. The slave became the asset to back the securities, which were added to a portfolio in which investors from both Europe and the United States could invest and mitigate their risks. Hart captures this mechanism: "Enslavers and speculators also securitized enslaved people in a manner that spread the vast wealth generated by enslaved labor well beyond the South and the smaller circle of those who had a direct relationship to enslavement to beneficiaries throughout the North Atlantic. Enslaved black labor powered the global capitalist economy."[166] This is a stunning instance of the kinds of innovations being practiced on black bodies before being incorporated within standard capitalist policies across the globe.

Racialization plays a key role in the Christian West's self-understanding of its redemptive mission through colonial expansion, settler conquest of native peoples, and the incorporation of chattel slaves from Africa.[167] Redeeming the heathen through enslavement and the purification of both pain and work provided part of the conceptual justification for territorial conquest and with it the creation of plantation and *encomienda* systems. Cedric Robinson, among others, has argued that racialization in the West long preceded capitalism, and that the two should not be seen as coterminous although capitalism requires

163 Hart, "Constellations," 9.

164 Baptist, *Half Has Never Been Told*, 248.

165 Hart, "Constellations," 11.

166 Hart, "Constellations," 12.

167 See Amaryah Shaye Armstrong, "Christian Order and Racial Order: What Cedric Robinson Has to Teach Us Today," *The Bias Magazine* June 3 (2020), https://christiansocialism.com/cedric-robinson-racial-order-christianity-socialism/.

and makes central use of racial categories.[168] As I have argued elsewhere, there is a longstanding logic evident within Christian thought that links theologies of redemption to payment, exchange, debt-based entrapment, and the obligated labor that results.[169] Marking the "barbarian" and racial others as demonic or at best as awaiting salvation allowed the pairing of the gospel proclamation with conquest, first within and at the borders of European Christendom and then extended into the New World.[170] Whether the heathen was actually redeemed or simply subdued and governed (and what better evidence for salvation is there than humble, industrious subjects?), such conquest was divine work.

The realities of racial capital and the racialization of labor and debt relations are gradually making their way into the consciousness of theological reflection. While typically acknowledging the realities of intersectionality, modern Christian thought has often approached economy as abstract and distinct from race and racism as essential and constitutive categories. Racialization of capital brings together race and class with attendant considerations of social reproduction that draw on gender and sexuality studies. Theologians have been addressing the role that religion has played in constructing and resisting this assemblage. It is important to consider the ways that theology has contributed to racial categories as well as upheld class and gender hierarchies.[171] Progressive theological responses have sought to provide frameworks for understanding God and theology from the point of view of marginal communities including people of color, the differently abled, and sexual minorities who have typically been othered and excluded from religious communities. Considering the racialization of capital together with social reproduction invites analyses of theology's role in maintaining or subverting the social, racial, and sexual contracts; protecting capital and asset transfer through patriarchal laws of inheritance; the policing of women's bodies around matters of

168 Robinson, *Black Marxism*; Cedric Robinson, *An Anthropology of Marxism* (New York: Ashgate, 2001).

169 Singh, *Divine Currency*, 166–192.

170 See, e.g., Eleanor Craig, "We Have Never Been Human/e: The Laws of Burgos and the Philosophy of Coloniality in the Americas," in *Beyond Man: Race, Coloniality, and Philosophy of Religion*, ed. Yountae An and Eleanor Craig (Durham, NC: Duke University Press, 2021).

171 J. Kameron Carter, *Race: A Theological Account* (New York: Oxford University Press, 2008); Willie James Jennings, *The Christian Imagination: Theology and the Origins of Race* (New Haven, CT: Yale University Press, 2010); Terence Keel, *Divine Variations: How Christian Thought Became Racial Science* (Stanford: Stanford University Press, 2018); Katie Walker Grimes, *Christ Divided: Antiblackness as Corporate Vice* (Minneapolis, MN: Fortress Press, 2017).

reproduction and childbearing; and other matters related to so-called human capital and labor that are always raced and gendered.

One key site of inquiry for the economic aspects of racialization, and in particular the status of antiblackness within the US, is the question of reparations. There is a strong theological and ethical case to be made for the justice of compensation, that those who have been wronged or exploited should have those wrongs corrected in a variety of ways including compensation. Since one of the driving factors for the success of capitalism was an abundance of free labor, repaying such labor is one step in addressing the injustice of the system. While the founding violence of capitalism and its past history cannot be undone, one clear step toward amelioration would be to provide compensation to the descendants of those who were robbed of their labor as well as denied the opportunity to hold wealth or own and transfer assets. The disproportionate level of poverty and the gross economic inequalities experienced by the American Black community are tied directly to a history of legal provisions denying access to or the transfer of capital. Theological and ethical reasoning might clarify that such compensation addresses the material value of the labor due and is not a form of moral atonement by white America or an appeasement to induce forgiveness on the part of Black folk.

3.7 *Social Reproduction, Affective Labor, and Care Work*

While unwaged, racialized slave labor served as the foundational shadow side at the peripheries of emerging global capitalism, a no less central form of unwaged labor serves as capitalism's hearth and home. Social reproduction names a host of essential yet repressed or ignored dynamics that reproduce the economic system and the laborer in any given mode of production. Typically, in capitalism, focus remains on the laborer's interface with a capitalist/employer. Here the wage relationship is key and paid – or at least priced – labor is the index of value. What is taken as producing value is the expenditure of labor time while at work. Yet "living labor" is a larger category and includes not simply the efforts at production of commodities but the efforts to reproduce the laboring class.[172] The time spent between work hours, time at home recuperating and engaging in relational, affective, and psychic activity, is just as essential to the maintenance of the economic system.

Classical construals of political economy and early Marxist responses were highly gendered. The figure of the worker was male and the labor of the

172 On living labor as a category see Enrique Dussel, *Towards an Unknown Marx: A Commentary on the Manuscripts of 1861–63*, trans. Yolanda Angulo (London: Routledge, 2001).

woman in the domestic sphere was forgotten or excluded from analysis.[173] Yet extensive amounts of unwaged and therefore invisible labor falls to (typically female) laborers in such spaces: work providing meals and comfort for weary laborers, work bearing and raising children, work providing elder care – all of which includes the procurement and preparation of material goods and sustenance and the provision of affective and emotional support. The important tradition of Marxist feminism has challenged the myopia of Marxian analysis in this regard, and other critical theorists are elevating a focus on social reproduction as essential.[174]

Because of the implicit and explicit gendering of social relations around labor, as well as the central role that biological reproduction plays in sustaining the system, social reproduction invites economic analyses in terms of gender and sexuality. This means that Christian thought engaging this question can draw on feminist, womanist, and queer theologies, for instance, in evaluating and constructing responses to such dynamics. That much invisible labor in the developed world falls on Black and Brown women's bodies also necessitates racial, ethnic, and post/decolonial critiques.[175]

One of several lines of response for Christian thought is an ethic of care, which ties in directly with matters of affective labor and care work and implicates the social reproductive system that sustains the economy.[176] The ethics of care is an approach that centers relational existence and assesses morality in terms of one's fulfillment of various relational obligations. It focuses on the needs and concerns of those with whom one is relationally connected, emphasizing the particularity of the needs of others in their specific social and historical contexts. Virginia Held, whose work systematically outlines a philosophy of care, presents the care of a child as a paradigm for such concerns.[177]

173 Katrine Marçal, *Who Cooked Adam Smith's Dinner? A Story about Women and Economics*, trans. Saskia Vogel (London: Portobello Books, 2015); Federici, *Caliban and the Witch.*

174 Silvia Federici, *Wages Against Housework* (Bristol, UK: Falling Wall Press and the Power of Women Collective, 1975); Tithi Bhattacharya, *Social Reproduction Theory: Remapping Class, Recentring Oppression* (London: Pluto Press, 2017); Nancy Fraser, "Contradictions of Capital and Care," *New Left Review* 100 (2016).

175 Central in this arena is Marcella Althaus-Reid, *Indecent Theology: Theological Perversions in Sex, Gender and Politics* (London: Routledge, 2000); Marcella Althaus-Reid, *From Feminist Theology to Indecent Theology: Readings on Poverty, Sexual Identity and God* (London: SCM Press, 2004).

176 See reflections on tenderness and care in Marcella Althaus-Reid, "Queering the Cross: The Politics of Redemption and the External Debt," *Feminist Theology* 15, no. 3 (2007).

177 Virginia Held, *The Ethics of Care: Personal, Political, and Global* (Oxford: Oxford University Press, 2006). See also Nel Noddings, *Caring: A Feminine Approach to Ethics & Moral*

Acting morally and ethically in such a scenario attends to vulnerability, affective bonds, relations of mutual dependence, and other senses of obligation that may precede and exceed universalized, abstract, or systemic construals of the ethical.

While the child provides an exemplary case, an ethics of care is not to be relegated simply to the familial, personal, or private sphere, but has bearing on broader publics including the national and international level. It also bears on matters of justice, and while care and justice cannot be collapsed together, they refine and shape one another in significant ways.[178] Care and concern for specificity of actors and contexts will emphasize restorative and redistributive forms of justice more than retributive. Beyond models of simple fairness or balance, care will emphasize corrective and ameliorative measures that may look imbalanced when contextual differences are ignored. Thus, while incorporating and attending to domestic and personal spaces, as much social reproduction theory does, the end result does not remain relegated to such "margins" but rather shows forth the essential nature of the system and offers broad, politically and socially relevant solutions.

An ethic of care emphasizes relational existence and eschews individualism. Not only does ethical formation not happen in isolation but the ethical as such is relational. In attending to the specificity and particularity of ethical others, the ethics of care challenge abstract and universal, one-size-fits all ethical models. Broadly prescribed, universalizable courses of action risk removing the ethical actor from history, society, and culture – not to mention biographical particularities including race, class, gender, and sexuality. Rather, an ethics of care emphasizes that moral action necessarily varies across time and space, that context and the specific needs of the other dictate what the ethical looks like in each situation. Furthermore, religiously inflected ethics of care derive injunctions to care for the poor and vulnerable from religious traditions in ways that resonate powerfully with the normative vision of this ethical system.

Given its attunement to relational dynamics and the variability emerging from specific relational encounters, an ethics of care is particularly suited to concerns about inequality.[179] In this regard, an ethics of care calls for attention

---

Education, 2nd ed. (Berkeley: University of California Press, 2003); Carol Gilligan, *In a Different Voice: Psychological Theory and Women's Development*, New ed. (Cambridge, MA: Harvard University Press, 1993).

178 Michael Slote, *The Ethics of Care and Empathy* (London: Routledge, 2007).

179 I explore care in relation to exchange, debt, and visions of the commons in Devin Singh, "Introduction Part II: Debt, Obligation, and Care on the Commons," in *Reimagining*

and concern for the classes rendered vulnerable or precarious. Moves toward restoration and redistribution will also challenge the differences and disparities in economic power and privilege. At the same time, an ethics of care recognizes particularity and the unique differences of those within social networks. This means the vision need not entail the erasure of qualitative differences such as divisions of labor, but seeks to rectify quantitative differences where some are barred from access to the goods of life. Theologies drawing on care theory, care work, and related notions of affect are emerging and engaging this important nexus of concerns.[180]

3.8 *Bureaucracy*

While we can find ample reflection on the nature of ecclesial hierarchy and the roles and offices of the church, the topic of bureaucracy, as such, has rarely been touched upon within theology or religious studies. Yet, there exists examination of bureaucracy not only within the modern social sciences but throughout the history of many human societies. Humans within complex civilizations have long been fascinated with and concerned about the implications of governance and social organization in terms of layers of complexity and distance, and the forms of occlusion and abuse that might result. Bureaucracy brings with it defined roles and the fixation of particular positions and offices, as well as chains of communication that are often opaque to outsiders, and yet operate according to a strict, internal, procedural logic.

While Max Weber is perhaps most well-known for studies of bureaucracy and its relation to rationalization, bureaucracy is not simply a modern phenomenon and need not be linked exclusively with theories of modernization and supposed disenchantment.[181] There is a rich anthropological literature on bureaucratic culture that complexifies early interventions such as Weber's with analyses of audits, archives, writing, and governance, for instance.[182] We also

---

Leadership on the Commons: Shifting the Paradigm for a More Ethical, Equitable, and Just World, ed. Devin Singh, Randal Joy Thompson, and Kathleen A. Curran (Bingley, UK: Emerald, 2021).

180 E.g., Karen Bray and Stephen D. Moore, eds., *Religion, Emotion, Sensation: Affect Theories and Theologies*, Transdisciplinary Theological Colloquia (New York: Fordham University Press, 2019); Karen Bray, *Grave Attending: A Political Theology for the Unredeemed* (New York: Fordham University Press, 2020).

181 Max Weber, *Economy and Society: An Outline of Interpretive Sociology* (Berkeley: University of California Press, 1978).

182 See, e.g., Marilyn Strathern, *Audit Cultures: Anthropological Studies in Accountability, Ethics, and the Academy*, European Association of Social Anthropologists (London: Routledge, 2000); Ashley Lebner, *Redescribing Relations: Strathernian Conversations on Ethnography, Knowledge and Politics* (New York: Berghahn Books, 2017).

find reflection on bureaucracy in ancient Greek and Roman sources, where writers express a desire for rulers to be seen and remain accessible, and a concern that they might not.[183] Richard Seaford and Marc Shell have explored the phenomenon of the hidden or occluded ruler or deity in archaic and ancient Greek sources.[184]

Both Shell and Seaford also suggest that the hierarchical and centralized institutional structures that characterize bureaucracy have much to do with a monetary economy. The kinds of agreements and decisions that might take place in bureaucratic organizations often require communication across distances and in absentia, along with record-keeping policies. Writing and money provide precisely such record keeping, tabulation, and communication opportunities that allow actors to interact without being face-to-face. Herodotus, for instance, describes Deiokes the Mede as one of the first to establish the rule that a governed people would only deal with the king through messengers and his representatives, and that the king would be inaccessible, hidden behind labyrinthine palace walls. Here we have a literal instantiation of the anxieties about the layers and barriers of bureaucracy that impede direct access to and communication with a sovereign. Deiokes rules with a harsh, calculative, rational justice and does so while hidden within the confines of his palace.[185]

Bureaucracy has been an element of human civilization since the rise of complex agrarian command economies in the ancient Near East, with their temple-palace resource complexes, tabulation systems for the allocation of grain, and the capture and sequestering of human capital through enforced labor and debt slavery.[186] Yet, bureaucracy certainly increases in complexity and preponderance in modernity. Technologies such as the printing press and the development of long-distance bills of exchange, or proto-paper currency,

---

183 Kathryn A. Morgan, ed., *Popular Tyranny: Sovereignty and its Discontents in Ancient Greece* (Austin: University of Texas Press, 2003).

184 Richard Seaford, "Tragic Tyranny," in *Popular Tyranny: Sovereignty and its Discontents in Ancient Greece*, ed. Kathryn A. Morgan (Austin: University of Texas Press, 2003); Shell, *The Economy of Literature*.

185 Herodotus, *Histories* 1:96–101; see the discussion in Shell, *Economy of Literature*.

186 Michael Hudson and Marc Van de Mieroop, eds., *Debt and Economic Renewal in the Ancient Near East* (Bethesda, MD: CDL Press, 2002); Michael Hudson and Cornelia Wunsch, eds., *Creating Economic Order: Record-Keeping, Standardization, and the Development of Accounting in the Ancient Near East* (Bethesda, MD: CDL Press, 2004); James C. Scott, *Against the Grain: A Deep History of the Earliest States* (New Haven: Yale University Press, 2017); Roland Boer, "Biting the Poor: On the Differences between Credit and Debt in Ancient Israel and Southwest Asia," *Journal of Religion and Society* 16 (2014); Roland Boer, "Reconsidering Debt Remission in Light of the Ancient World," *Continental Thought and Theory* 1, no. 2 (2017).

accelerate the capacities for bureaucracy in light of its reliance on both writing and money. The printing press enabled greater forms of record keeping, and paper currency facilitated exchange at a distance according to agreements set between various accounts and under the watchful eye of sovereignty as soon as it incorporated paper currency into its fiat monetary system. We see as well the increase in surveillance capacities, a focus on the archive, and the control of the body through forms of criminal record keeping, whether in written or photographic technological modes.[187] These are all manifestations of and extensions of hierarchy and bureaucracy within institutional systems.

The early Christian theologian Pseudo-Dionysius famously expounded upon celestial and ecclesial hierarchies, exploring the layers of churchly and heavenly authority, representation, and mediation between human and divine.[188] Giorgio Agamben, among others, has taken up reflection on this theme in Christian thought to expound on angelology as a kind of heavenly bureaucracy.[189] While dramatically evident in Pseudo-Dionysius, a majority of Christian theologians across the centuries exhibit concern over questions of representation, mediation, and distance between God and creation, whether or not angelic beings or other mediators are also considered.

Such conceptual elaborations are ways to think about governance, leadership, and social organization. One could also read them as the projection and working out of anxieties about such complexity and power relations onto celestial bodies. Such projection is in part a way to allay anxieties about such forms of governance through the legitimation provided by a heavenly model. To ascribe order and hierarchy to the heavens allows for humans under certain forms of control to feel at peace with or at least reconcile themselves to such subjugation.

Furthermore, one interpretation of the cross event, and certainly one championed by Martin Luther, emphasized the "tearing of the veil" and direct access to God the heavenly sovereign, expressing a longing to overcome bureaucratic

187 Michel Foucault, *Discipline and Punish: The Birth of the Prison*, 2nd ed. (New York: Vintage Books, 1995); Allan Sekula, "The Body and Archive," *October* 39 (1986).

188 Pseudo-Dionysius the Areopagite, *On the Ecclesiastical Hierarchy* and *On the Celestial Hierarchy*.

189 Giorgio Agamben, *The Kingdom and the Glory: For a Theological Genealogy of Economy and Government*, trans. Lorenzo Chiesa and Matteo Mandarini (Stanford: Stanford University Press, 2011); Giorgio Agamben, *Die Beamten des Himmels: Über Engel*, trans. Andreas Hiepko (Berlin: Verlag der Weltreligionen im Insel Verlag, 2007). Compare also David Newheiser, "Desacralizing Political Theology: Dionysius the Areopagite and Giorgio Agamben," *Modern Theology* 36, no. 1 (2020); David Newheiser, *Hope in a Secular Age: Deconstruction, Negative Theology and the Future of Faith* (Cambridge: Cambridge University Press, 2019).

distance. Just like the proverbial desire to "talk directly to someone in charge" and have our needs and concerns heeded and taken care of by the one with the power and authority to address them, here there is a desire to overcome the barriers of priests and other mediators, in order to have one's concerns dealt with at the heavenly throne, cutting through layers of spiritual and celestial red tape. Luther makes this explicit with his extensive critique of the Roman Catholic church's own layers of bureaucratic control and the corruption that he claimed was festering within the hierarchy.[190]

Such concerns remain present today in our critique of corporations and the anger and distrust that we as consumers feel about powerful, faceless organizations and not having direct access to real decision-makers. Part of the frustration and resentment toward CEOs such as Jeff Bezos is not only their wealth and the inequality that they exemplify, but that they are figureheads or leaders of organizations that are opaque and yet exert influence and control over our lives. Such opacity and inordinate influence inspire religious imagery as a way to depict what exceeds the capacity for human perception and to suggest hidden influence.

Part of the appeal of the early Christian church and the Acts community to various radical reformers across Christian history has been the immediacy and lack of hierarchy and bureaucracy.[191] The organization appears flat and lacks layers. Governance appears egalitarian. It exemplifies a kind of freedom of assembly, communication, and decision-making. Constantinian Christendom is not simply critiqued for the wedding of the church to imperial power but for the complexity and layers of church authority that proliferate in concert with imperial institutions and their bureaucracies.

At the same time, it must be acknowledged that many find comfort in the sense of order provided by defined roles, with their attendant hierarchies and senses of bureaucratic control. Part of the appeal of so-called traditional ecclesiological or "high church" structures may in fact be the security of bureaucracy, order, and defined processes. Certainly this affinity lives on in contemporary forms of technocracy and the anxiety-allaying possibilities projected by total planning in systems of governance. One stereotype of contemporary party politics is that, inasmuch as the right desires a singular strongman to lead and

190 See esp. Martin Luther, *The Freedom of a Christian* and *The Babylonian Captivity of the Church*.

191 See, e.g., Jan Hus, *The Letters of John Hus* (London: Hodder and Stoughton, 1904); Gerrard Winstanley et al., *The True Levellers Standard Advanced, or, The State of Community Opened, and Presented to the Sons of Men* (London 1649).

guide them, much of the left desires more extensive planning and systemic control for a similar sense of reassurance.

These dynamics raise questions about the association of bureaucracy with ritual. The ritual process includes the navigation of liminality and uncertainty, the creation of arbitrary lines and boundaries, the prohibition to cross such lines, as well as often the intentional transgression of such lines, coupled with additional means to atone for and deal with such planned or contrived transgressions. Ritual may involve defined roles and positions as well, and may include forms of opacity and privileged means of communication. There is a logic and order to the ritual process.[192] Rituals are also an effort to mitigate chance and contingency.[193]

Such elements can be discerned in bureaucracy, and bureaucracy can be posited as a structure within organizations containing their stipulated rituals and forging ritual cultures. Because there is an economy of exchange within ritual, these dynamics also link up with our discussion of economy as well as with the connections among money, written record keeping, and bureaucratic structures. Thus, much fruitful work remains to be done to explore reflections on bureaucracy that are often implicit within Christian thought. Light needs to be shed on the direct critiques of and in some cases praise and support for bureaucratic structures within ecclesiology and other sectors of Christian theology. The need also extends to types of Christian critique of or support for bureaucracy in wider society.

3.9 *Corporate Form*

Related to bureaucracy but necessitating a distinct site of inquiry are questions surrounding the origins and genealogy of the corporation and its links with Christian thought and practice. While the corporate form can be taken in its broadest possible sense, from various types of incorporation in the body politic, church, and other organizations, I have in view here a more narrow connotation associated with "the firm" and business enterprise. The history of the business corporation must be thought together with the history of the body politic, emerging notions of nationhood, and the vicissitudes of ecclesiastical

192 On ritual see, e.g., Victor Turner, *The Ritual Process: Structure and Anti-Structure*, The Lewis Henry Morgan Lectures (Chicago: Aldine, 1969); Catherine M. Bell, *Ritual: Perspectives and Dimensions* (New York: Oxford University Press, 1997); Catherine M. Bell, *Ritual Theory, Ritual Practice* (New York, NY: Oxford University Press, 1992); on arbitraty rites of institution, see Pierre Bourdieu, *The Logic of Practice* (Stanford: Stanford University Press, 1990).

193 Ramey, *Politics of Divination*.

structure in the West. The corporation is also related to notions of personhood, embodiment, time, and other metaphysical concerns.[194]

During his 2011 presidential bid, Mitt Romney was heckled by protestors while stumping at the Iowa State Fair. While defending his position not to raise taxes, someone in the crowd shouted out "Corporations!" presumably highlighting various loopholes that significantly reduce a firm's tax liability. Romney's retort quickly became a thing of modest legend: "Corporations are people, my friend!" The crowd was stunned and in the brief exchange that followed, Romney elaborated: "Everything corporations earn ultimately goes to people." His point was that raising taxes on corporations amounts to raising taxes on the people that make them up and is thus unproductive.[195] Romney's explanation was soon forgotten, but his initial reply made the media rounds and was lampooned by his critics. Ironically, it was this initial statement that was closer to the truth. While it is highly tendentious to equate the tax impact on corporations with the tax impact on individuals, it is in fact the case that, legally speaking, corporations are people. This concept has a theological genealogy.

Pope Innocent IV coined the term *persona ficta* in 1243 to designate legally created fictitious persons, which was a category eventually applied to business corporations.[196] He used the term in two practical instances: the first upheld the possibility that a formal assembly of individuals could swear an oath as a group and be bound by it, since for legal purposes the group could be compelled as a fictitious singular entity. The second case denied the possibility that a corporation could be excommunicated, recognizing that legal personhood in this case could not be extended to matters of the soul and sacrament.[197] He thus provided a basis for and sense of limits to the notion of legal personhood for formal group associations that has since been expounded and amplified in various contexts. As sociologist James Coleman recounts,

---

194 See Perry Dane, "Corporations," in *The Routledge Handbook of Economic Theology*, ed. Stefan Schwarzkopf (London: Routledge, 2020). For a charge to examine the corporate form in non-Western, non-Christian contexts, see Levi McLaughlin et al., "Why Scholars of Religion Must Investigate the Corporate Form," *Journal of the American Academy of Religion* 88, no. 3 (2020). One key study is Amanda Porterfield, *Corporate Spirit: Religion and the Rise of the Modern Corporation* (Oxford: Oxford University Press, 2018). See also Lofton, *Consuming Religion*; McCarraher, *Enchantments of Mammon*, 177–254.

195 Philip Rucker, "Mitt Romney Says 'Corporations Are People'," *Washington Post*, August 11, 2011.

196 See discussion in Otto Gierke, *Political Theories of the Middle Age*, trans. Frederic William Maitland (Cambridge: Cambridge University Press, 1900).

197 These cases are reviewed in Maximilian Koessler, "The Person in Imagination or Persona Ficta of the Corporation," *Louisiana Law Review* 9, no. 4 (1949): 437–39.

> This new legal form was widely used in England in the fourteenth century, where boroughs gaining charters from the King came into legal personhood. These boroughs (such as Cambridge, which received a charter of sorts from King John in the twelfth century) paved the way for the great trading companies of the seventeenth and eighteenth centuries (such as the East India Company) and more generally for the modern corporation and voluntary associations of all varieties.[198]

For Coleman, the corporation was distinct from what he terms "primordial" organizations like the family or church. It represented the formal creation of "purposive" organizations that transformed society and ushered in modernity through a kind of rational reconstruction. Whether we accept this distinction and causality, the corporation represents a watershed development in legal theory that has implications for business and economy directly, but also for religion, politics, and social organization. Not only does it raise ethical questions about the best structures for and activities of corporations, but it raises metaphysical and other abstract philosophical questions about personhood and subjectivity. Just as the individual self was being redefined and "buffered" in modernity, corporate selves were taking on new levels of agency and exerting influence on national and global scales.[199]

Genealogically, there were theological and specifically ecclesiological sources of the conceptual fodder for the corporate form. Some of these have as their background ideas of incorporation into the body of Christ and the church as the ideal corporate form. They draw on the complexities of belonging while maintaining individual identity, which preoccupied authors reflecting on the unity and distinction within the body of Christ as established in Pauline thought.[200] These ecclesiological concerns themselves were grafted onto preexisting concerns about how to model the body politic, and in the Middle Ages they manifested in new ideas about the fictious body of the king, which was transposed onto the body of the commonwealth of royal subjects. These developments can be traced in the permutations of the *corpus mysticum* of the body of Christ, first as the literal body of the savior, then the corporate body of the

198 James Coleman, "The Rational Reconstruction of Society: 1992 Presidential Address," *American Sociological Review* 58, no. 1 (1993): 2.

199 On the modern, buffered self, see Charles Taylor, *A Secular Age* (Cambridge, MA: Belknap Press of Harvard University Press, 2007).

200 See Devin Singh, "Until We Are One? Biopolitics and the United Body," in *'In Christ' in Paul: Explorations in Paul's Theology of Union and Participation*, ed. Kevin J. Vanhoozer, Constantine R. Campbell, and Michael J. Thate, WUNT/II (Tuebingen: Mohr Siebeck, 2014).

church, at times to the sacramental body of the Eucharistic host, and then as projected onto the political body of the state.[201]

These issues served as central conceptual points for thinking about the church as an institution as well as about society under Christendom as a body politic modeled on the church. There was no stopping the influence of such theorizations to help imagine other institutional forms. While merchants long preceded the emergence of Christianity, the merchant was a key site of contention within Christendom. The relationship among the merchants and the societies of traders in Europe, themselves providing significant wealth to the church, needed to be further theologically refined and ethically located. Amid the ferment of new economic reflection around usury and moneylending came new ideas of the "just merchant" and what it meant to engage in fair exchange under the eyes of God.[202] The forms of association and partnership that were licit and that kept with scriptural and scholastic interpretation in the Catholic West contributed to new legal forms that framed business arrangements over the long term. The quest for permanence and stability, particularly during the tumultuous political history of Europe in the Middle Ages, gave rise to such conceptual forms and their attendant legal frameworks.

One of the major reasons for the birth of the corporation in its modern form was the problem of death, taking us into theological and philosophical territory. The corporate form was created to be an eternal being – or, at least, one whose life-span extended beyond the typical life-span of a human and could overcome the problem of historical finitude. The corporation never dies but is a legal person that may carry on across the chasm normally marked by death. Just as the king's body never died but was transformed and transmuted, thinkers around the corporation gestured to notions of perpetuity and existential permanence in order to preserve capital, assets, and institutional structures across time and history. Ventures could be entered into, wealth accumulated, and claims made that could stand the test of time and be projected beyond the death of original members of a corporation. Arguably this vision was inspired by Christian imagination about the perpetuity and eternal destiny of the

201 Ernst Kantorowicz, *The King's Two Bodies: A Study in Medieval Political Theology* (Princeton, NJ: Princeton University Press, 1957).

202 Giacomo Todeschini, "Theological Roots of the Medieval/Modern Merchants' Self-Representation," in *The Self-Perception of Early Modern "Capitalists"*, ed. Margaret C. Jacob and Catherine Secretan (New York: Palgrave-MacMillan, 2008); Giacomo Todeschini, *Les Marchands et le Temple: La société chrétienne et le cercle vertueux de la richesse du Moyen Âge à l'Epoque moderne*, trans. Ida Giordano and Mathieu Arnoux (Paris: Albin Michel, 2017); Paolo Santori, "Was Aquinas a 'Universal Economist'?," *History of Economics Review* 72, no. 1 (2019).

church as the body of Christ. Such tactics of negotiating mortality and finitude invite theological assessments of the corporate person.

The fact that the corporate person or *persona ficta* is a legal entity offers one of many possible sites of analysis of the interaction among law, politics, and economy. Encoding the corporation in legal structures and enforcing such existence through the coercion of the state shows the necessity of the state institution in regulating and promoting market interactions. In addition to exploding the mythology of the spontaneous and self-regulating market, this allows for political theological analyses of the kinds of sovereignties delegated and deputized to corporations through the authorization of the state. The parallel development of the corporate form in relation to the king's two bodies allows for historical and genealogical investigations into the political theology of corporations. In other words, the corporation is not simply a site for economic theological analysis but fully political theological inquiries as well.

In relation to the question of sovereignty and tying back to the previous discussion of bureaucracy, many contemporary corporations attempt to be anti-bureaucratic and style themselves in opposition to complex (and presumably inefficient) state institutions. Many organizational theories currently embrace consensus models and flat, egalitarian administrative practices. Hierarchy and centralization are thus not necessarily coincidental with the corporate form, despite a long history of such overlap.[203]

This invites more nuanced assessment of sovereignty and its relation to governmentality, understood as dispersed forms of surveillance, policing, and normativity that eschew more openly coercive modes of oversight and centralization.[204] This does not take us outside the realm of power and its forms of open and covert influence, but it calls for different conceptual frameworks. While, at times, the corporate form appears to resonate with centralized forms of decision and top-down models, this does not exhaust the styles of leadership that corporations manifest. The recent political moment (2016–2020)

203 See, e.g., David Ellerman, "The Democratic Firm: An Argument Based on Ordinary Jurisprudence," *Journal of Business Ethics* 21, no. 2 (1999); Herminia Ibarra and Morten T. Hansen, "Are You a Collaborative Leader?," *Harvard Business Review*, July–August 2011, https://hbr.org/2011/07/are-you-a-collaborative-leader.

204 Graham Burchell, Colin Gordon, and Peter Miller, eds., *The Foucault Effect: Studies in Governmentality* (Chicago: University of Chicago Press, 1991); Michel Foucault, *Society Must Be Defended: Lectures at the Collège de France, 1975–76*, ed. Mauro Bertani, et al. (New York: Picador, 2003); Michel Foucault, *Security, Territory, Population: Lectures at the Collège de France, 1977–1978*, ed. Michel Senellart and Arnold I. Davidson (New York: Palgrave Macmillan, 2007); Mitchell Dean, *Governmentality: Power and Rule in Modern Society*, 2nd ed. (London: SAGE, 2010).

within the United States also shows the merger of corporatist practices with forms of centralized sovereignty in complex ways that escape easy categorization. Having a supposedly successful businessman as president might lead to innovation and a consensus style of leadership that takes place in many corporations. And yet it led to autocracy and forms of old-school dictatorship, smacking of a bygone era of corporate leadership practices.

A variety of directions present themselves for Christian thought to engage in an analysis of the corporate form. The most obvious are ethical concerns about the practices of corporations in terms of how they engage with society, how they treat their employees and the public, how they interact with and avoid legal regulations, and the kinds of direct impact they have through advertising and marketing. Concerns about consumption and commodification center on corporate practices as well, as the drivers and architects of such practices. While corporations certainly include the older industrial model and Fordist labor patterns, modern corporate labor is marked by a shift to white collar knowledge work. This raises questions about labor relations and labor justice as well as workplace practices that include and exclude various bodies. The shift to a heavy infrastructure of managerial elites as well as increasing levels of administrative bloat and complexity raise further concerns.

In addition, based on the theological genealogy recounted here, the interaction between the business corporation and the church is a site of interest. This is most obvious within contemporary megachurch studies, where evangelical and other nondenominational churches emulate corporate practices of leadership, media communication, and even financial accountancy.[205] The "Purpose Driven Life" and "Purpose Driven Church" coincide with "Jesus as CEO," all intermeshing in pastoral management practices that interact with corporate leadership principles.[206] The leadership gurus who advise CEOs are often (former) pastors who bring Christian insights into the boardroom, while

205 Henry Farnham May, *Protestant Churches and Industrial America* (New York: Harper, 1949); Thomas C. Leonard, "Religion and Evolution in Progressive Era Political Economy: Adversaries or Allies?," *History of Political Economy* 43, no. 3 (2011); James S. Bielo, "'The Mind of Christ': Financial Success, Born-again Personhood, and the Anthropology of Christianity," *Ethnos* 72, no. 3 (2007); Jon Bialecki, "Between Stewardship and Sacrifice: Agency and Economy in a Southern California Charismatic Church," *Journal of the Royal Anthropological Institute* 14, no. 2 (2008); Caitlin Zaloom, "The Evangelical Financial Ethic: Doubled Forms and the Search for God in the Economic World," *American Ethnologist* 43, no. 2 (2016).

206 Rick Warren, *The Purpose Driven Church: Growth Without Compromising Your Message & Mission* (Grand Rapids, MI: Zondervan, 1995); Rick Warren, *The Purpose-Driven Life: What on Earth am I Here For?* (Grand Rapids, MI: Zondervan, 2002); Laurie Beth Jones, *Jesus,*

in turn importing corporate practices into the church.[207] The interchange of corporate and ecclesial practices thus invites further study to complement studies of the role of Christian businessmen's associations and other initiatives of Christian entrepreneurship that enthusiastically endorse capitalist work culture and practices.

3.10 *Consumption and Commodification*

Critiques of consumption, consumerism, and commodification emerge often in the encounter between Christian thought and economy.[208] Such approaches often follow a line of analysis informed by Marx's critique of commodity fetishism and at times correlated to Gilles Deleuze and Félix Guattari's explorations of the disciplining of desire under capitalism.[209] Theologians and ethicists have analyzed the varying ways market forces and advertising tactics produce consumers. They contrast these directions of desire with the supposedly different patterns of desire shaped by theology and life in the Christian church. Their view is that there is something perverse and misdirected in worldly desires and that market culture exacerbates these tendencies, doubling down on such misdirection for the sake of profit. This interpretation often follows a line of thought from Augustine of Hippo, whose reflections on rightly ordered loves and the misdirection of desire under sin have fueled extensive examination of the topic.

According to many modern presentations of the dangers of consumption, healing and restoration, not to mention liberation, come from refashioning one's desires within Christian community. This refashioning centers around practices that are theologically framed, with different ends (e.g., love of neighbor and the worship, glorification, and enjoyment of God) that direct desire heavenward. One strand of such scholarship emphasizes liturgy and especially

CEO: Using Ancient Wisdom for Visionary Leadership, 25th Anniv. ed. (New York: Hachette Go, 2021).

207 Arguably, the most successful exemplar is bestselling author and speaker John Maxwell. See, e.g., John C. Maxwell, *The 21 Irrefutable Laws of Leadership: Follow Them and People will Follow You*, Rev. and updated 10th anniv. ed. (Nashville, TN: Thomas Nelson, 2007).

208 Robert Wuthnow, ed., *Rethinking Materialism: Perspectives on the Spiritual Dimension of Economic Behavior* (Grand Rapids, MI: Eerdmans, 1995); Vincent Miller, *Consuming Religion: Christian Faith and Practice in a Consumer Culture* (New York: Continuum, 2004); Kenneth R. Himes, "Consumerism and Christian Ethics," *Theological Studies* 68, no. 1 (2007); Cavanaugh, *Being Consumed*; Daniel M. Bell, *The Economy of Desire: Christianity and Capitalism in a Postmodern World* (Grand Rapids, MI: Baker Academic, 2012).

209 Marx, *Capital*, vol. 1; Gilles Deleuze and Félix Guattari, *Anti-Oedipus: Capitalism and Schizophrenia* (Minneapolis: University of Minnesota Press, 1983).

the Eucharist. Such reasoning asserts that regular participation in such rituals retrains and refashions mindsets, bodies, and desires, enabling critical distance from the patterns of consumption established as the norm by the world. Another strand emphasizes acts of service and solidarity with others, particularly fellow believers or the poor and marginalized. Here it is realignment with those excluded from the system that enables one to depart from the patterns of uncritical consumerism followed by society at large. These approaches thus combine analyses of desire, embodiment, and particular horizons of orientation, contrasting worldly or secular practices that have been colonized by the market with Christian ones that purportedly offer respite.

One interesting recent development in this area consists of studies problematizing the valorization of Christian practices as a panacea to consumerism. Such approaches, such as Lauren Winner's, might recall the ways Christian practices such as the Eucharist have been used as much to exclude and persecute as to include.[210] Others, such as Antonio Eduardo Alonso, might reflect on the ways Christian thought and practice around such sacraments have actually fueled market innovation around commodities.[211] Parallel investigations into the history of pilgrimage sites and the market around relics also challenge easy dichotomies of ostensibly pure and spiritual Christian spaces and depraved secular spaces of the market, showing instead that devotional activity and market activity frequently interpenetrate, and that Christian interventions have served to heighten as much as challenge consumptive activities over the centuries.[212]

3.11 *Gifts and Gifting*

Consumption is a matter of exchanges and one's disposition toward others and objects in such exchanges. As such, it relates to discussions about the gift and gifting in theology, philosophy, and the social sciences, which are widely developed and exceed the possibility of summation here.[213] The gift

210 Lauren F. Winner, *The Dangers of Christian Practice: On Wayward Gifts, Characteristic Damage, and Sin* (New Haven, CT: Yale University Press, 2018).

211 Antonio Eduardo Alonso, *Commodified Communion: Eucharist, Consumer Culture, and the Practice of Everyday Life* (New York: Fordham University Press, 2021).

212 Simon Coleman and John Eade, "Pilgrimage and Political Economy: Introduction to a Research Agenda," in *Pilgrimage and Political Economy: Translating the Sacred*, ed. Simon Coleman and John Eade (New York: Berghahn Books, 2018).

213 Among a plethora of possible sources, see Tanner, *Economy of Grace*; John Milbank, "Can a Gift Be Given? Prolegomena to a Future Trinitarian Metaphysic," *Modern Theology* 11, no. 1 (1995); Edith Wyschogrod, Jean-Joseph Goux, and Eric Boynton, eds., *The Enigma of Gift and Sacrifice*, Perspectives in Continental Philosophy (New York: Fordham University

has emerged within such discussions as a way to think about forms of reciprocity and exchange in connection to and offered in contrast with modern, capitalist, monetary economies. Spurred on by Marcel Mauss's seminal work on the gift, which explored the relationship between archaic and modern notions of exchange and obligation, theologians and ethicists have drawn on ideas of gifts from anthropology as well as biblical studies to articulate senses of exchange that appear best to articulate certain Christian ethical orientations. Quite often this involves claims about the kinds of exchanges that God is involved in, whether within Godself in a trinitarian economy, or between God and creation in terms of God's relationship as sovereign lord, father, mother, nurturer, friend, or another model whose metaphors and images engender certain assumptions about exchange relations.

The gift is often held up as a radical alternative to monetary and commodity-based exchanges, which are seen instead as ways to demarcate and track value as well as quantify relationships in ways that may be damaging.[214] The latter appear to partake of ideas of scarcity whereas the gift is seen as trading on abundance and open generosity. Gift language within Christian thought often overlaps with notions of divine grace and gratuity, also adding weight to such visions.

One of the challenges of drawing on the concept of the gift to articulate an ethical position is that the gift is a traveling signifier, a capacious concept whose content varies depending on the one describing it. The gift has been used to articulate sacrificial, other-oriented modes of giving that have no regard for return or reciprocity. Such views might take as their governing metaphor the

---

Press, 2002); John D. Caputo and Michael J. Scanlon, *God, the Gift, and Postmodernism* (Bloomington: Indiana University Press, 1999); John Barclay, *Paul and the Gift* (Grand Rapids, MI: Eerdmans, 2015); Thomas R. Blanton, *Spiritual Economy: Gift Exchange in the Letters of Paul of Tarsus*, Synkrisis (New Haven, CT: Yale University Press, 2017); Jean-Luc Marion, *Being Given: Toward a Phenomenology of Givenness* (Stanford: Stanford University Press, 2002). For a recent engagement with some of the philosophical debates on the gift, see Rose, *Theology of Failure*, 86–118.

214 Stark theological contrasts often rely on equally rigid anthropological demarcations of gifts versus commodities. See, e.g., C. A. Gregory, *Gifts and Commodities* (London: Academic Press, 1982). Challenges to this opposition include Caroline Humphrey and Stephen Hugh-Jones, *Barter, Exchange, and Value: An Anthropological Approach* (Cambridge: Cambridge University Press, 1992). It is important to note that anthropological descriptions may already be highly theologically laden and should not be taken as necessarily more objective or empirical foundations for subsequent theologizing. For a good exploration of the theological agendas of some key anthropologists of ritual, see Alonso, *Commodified Communion*.

notion of Christ's self-donation on the cross, which is seen as radically selfless and aimed to benefit humanity with no regard for a return to or gain on God's behalf. Others have noted that gifts within archaic communities, at least as described in anthropological accounts, do not appear to escape reciprocity and indeed often include stringent notions of obligation, whether to return counter gifts to the giver, or to "pay it forward" in alternative prestations to others within the community. Such insights have led to alternative construals of divine gifting, where God's calculated return is kept in view. Divine gifts often come with strings attached.

Reflection upon gift giving within both archaic and modern societies also signals the ways gifts are bound to questions of recognition, status, and honor, as well as alternative modes of expressing reciprocity and relational bonds.[215] To be sure, the gift in pre-industrial or premodern communities could be used to control and obligate, as lavish forms of generosity might overwhelm a recipient and prevent them from adequately reciprocating. Such moves are sometimes on display today as well. In such situations, the gift appears at best as a tool of control and at worst as a method of enslavement. Such scenarios resonate with and may even prefigure forms of debt slavery, where a gift or donation made is so great that the recipient has no possible way of reciprocating other than offering themselves as collateral, whether by means of labor (material or affective) or through other kinds of value in an effort to balance the scales.[216]

What is noteworthy in debates around the gift is what these discussions signal about the kinds of ideals and virtues being sought within economic relations.[217] They similarly reveal the kinds of economic visions being charted from within various sectors of Christian thought. Regardless of whether it is gift, money, or other symbolic markers of exchange, we find virtues and values set

215 While sometimes overshadowed by discussion of objects or goods of exchange, it is important to keep in view that gifts can include services and other labor. The transformation of gift labor by the wage system is helpfully explored in Rachel Smith, "The Meaning of 'Free' Work: Service as a Gift, and Labor as a Commodity for Ni-Vanuatu Labor Migrants," in *Work, Society and the Ethical Self: Chimeras of Freedom in the Neoliberal Era*, ed. Chips Hann (New York: Berghahn Books, 2021).

216 For examples of slavery in pre- or non-monetary societies, see Kent V. Flannery and Joyce Marcus, *The Creation of Inequality: How our Prehistoric Ancestors set the Stage for Monarchy, Slavery, and Empire* (Cambridge, MA: Harvard University Press, 2012). For support for this account coupled with nuance and challenge, see now David Graeber and David Wengrow, *The Dawn of Everything: A New History of Humanity* (New York: Farrar, Straus and Giroux, 2021).

217 I explore this further in Singh, "Debt, Obligation, and Care on the Commons."

out such as generosity, selflessness, and other-focus; avoidance or diminution of profit or return; reduction of self-seeking motives; attention on the relationship as opposed to the exchange or its objects; exchanges that benefit long-term stability and community building over short-term gains in value; ways of tracking value that are flexible and qualitative as opposed to reductively quantitative and numerical; forms of value generation that remain within the community and are shared as opposed to hoarded or that lead to scarcity; non-competitive and mutually beneficial exchanges; giving in ways that maintain the dignity and value of both giver and receiver; forms of giving that are targeted, specific, and meet actual needs, and yet are also excessive in ways that signify love, abundant care, and concern; exchanges that are nonexploitative and nonextractive, that seek to ameliorate and address needs or provide security and stability as opposed to take advantage of the other party. The list could go on. Differing positions around the ethics of the gift appear as proxies for advancing various social ethics. While much heat and light have been generated by debates about the gift, such conversations should continue in an effort to construct preferable exchange relations and institutional arrangements.

3.12 *Digital Currencies and Cryptocurrencies*

New forms of technological innovation and mediation also mean changes for the nature of economic exchange and resulting implications for morality and ethics to which Christian thought might speak. Money itself is a technology, a radical one whose invention changed the course of human civilization. Human society as it evolved over the last five thousand years would be inconceivable without money. The digital revolution is its own technological watershed. The advent of the printing press, a radical technological advance in its own right, meant key changes in the possibilities for money, such as standardized, mass-produced banknotes. Likewise, the wedding of ancient monetary technologies with new digital forms of representation and information exchange mean new possibilities for money as well as new moral, philosophical, and theological challenges.

The fusion of money with digital technologies has resulted in innovations such as digital currencies and cryptocurrencies. While one could justifiably present digital currencies as the larger category within which cryptocurrencies are a subset, I intend to signal something different in this distinction. By digital currencies I mean sovereign currencies exchanged on digital platforms. Popular platforms include PayPal, Venmo, Zelle, and Cash App, for instance, which are fairly straightforward replacements for cash exchange that accomplish the same thing but remove the need for physical currency or face to face encounter. Yet there are a variety of other forms of exchange emerging in the digital sphere that offer apparent innovations brought on by digitization, such as plans by Facebook to issue its own currency modeled on fiat currency and (at least for now) pegged to the dollar. The category of digital currency allows us to explore what technological mediation and digitization do for monetary exchange even if such exchange is still within the bounds of conventionally accepted sovereign currencies. This is a key distinction from cryptocurrencies, which, as we will shortly consider, make their mark by attempting an alternative to sovereign currencies.

The advent of digital currencies raises the specter of dematerialization and has kindled for some observers either an anxiety or thrill about an imminent cashless society. Some posit this is a new manifestation of money. One then might wonder about the new social consciousness and novel politics that will emerge with it. While we must consider the impact of digitization, it is worth recalling that from a long historical view, this is not the first time that cashless societies have emerged. For millennia before the advent of coinage in ancient Lydia around 600 BCE, ancient Near Eastern empires established weights and measures and set price proportions for the exchange of goods, effectively creating what economic sociologist Geoffrey Ingham emphasizes was a "money of account."[218] The conceptual apparatus of money existed long before material tokens came to signify these sovereign denominations and circulate among a governed populace. That we tend to associate money with coins and other material tokens reflects the conceptual disciplining of centuries of practice with such tokens. In addition to this cashless prehistory, examples exist of communities where monetary tokens disappear, whether due to currency shortages or regime failure, and community members continue to exchange with denominations in the local currency while keeping track with ledgers or other tools.[219] In light of such historical variation, the current move to cashless transactions using digital markers appears less radical.

The fact that money has dematerialized at various points in its history does not mean, however, that digitization is insignificant. The medium brings new possibilities for exchange. The financial technology (fintech) industry is currently one of the fastest growing sectors and is awash with new applications that enable peer-to-peer lending and easier access to credit, for instance. Individuals are able to bypass large banks with unwieldy regulations and slow bureaucratic processes to access loans quickly at competitive rates. Marketing copy on Upstart's website, for instance, claims that "unless you're one of the few percent of Americans with significant wealth, the price of borrowing

218 Ingham, *The Nature of Money*.

219 Innes, "What Is Money?."; Graeber, *Debt: The First 5,000 Years*.

affects you every day. Throughout history, affordable credit has been central to unlocking mobility and opportunity."[220] Upstart bills itself as a company that unlocks credit options for more people at lower rates by using AI to calculate creditworthiness beyond traditional FICO scores. Another fintech company, Conductiv, uses machine learning to smooth transactions between would-be borrowers and lenders, whose credit approval process might introduce inefficiencies that screen out viable customers.[221] Other fintech innovations seek to broaden access to conventional monetary products, such as Robinhood's claim to be "on a mission to democratize finance for all" by making stock trading less costly and more accessible to non-specialists.[222] EarnUp claims to make mortgages more accessible by clarifying borrower risk to lenders through better predictive models and assessments.[223]

Such interventions are changing the nature and terms of lending relationships, raising questions about the new patterns of community and social organization that result. They certainly appear to be disseminating a digital "cash nexus," the increased mediation of social relations by money. This trend invites reflection on the ethical, theological, and philosophical implications for our understanding of relationships, family structures, and broader social formations and obligations. In an interview, Upstart cofounder and CEO Dave Girouard proclaims that the company helps "someone to borrow from their future selves" through a process of "monetizing future potential."[224] Such a dynamic appears to capture vividly what Maurizio Lazaratto has called the "indebted man," a subject whose future possibilities have been captured and delimited by debt.[225] Such broad-based subjective indebtedness has prompted Kathryn Tanner's recent intervention on theological anthropology to liberate the subject that is "chained to the past" by such debt instruments.[226]

Undoubtedly, more pragmatic and policy-minded ethicists might push back on such philosophical concerns and highlight the new opportunities afforded by approaches such as Upstart's, which provides access to credit that might not normally be available and thereby actually opens up future horizons already foreclosed due to the constraints of the current system. Others might weigh in on the ambivalences of inducting unbanked and underbanked communities into the financial system through more "democratized" forms of lending such

220 "About," Upstart.com, https://www.upstart.com/about#, accessed Nov. 19, 2020.

221 Conductiv.co, https://conductiv.co/, accessed Nov. 19, 2020.

222 "Careers," Robinhood.com, https://robinhood.com/us/en/careers/, accessed Nov. 19, 2020.

223 "Solutions," Earnup.com, https://earnup.com/solutions, accessed Nov. 19, 2020.

224 Larry Dignan, "Q&A: Upstart CEO Dave Girouard," ZDNet.com, May 16, 2013, https://www.zdnet.com/article/q-a-upstart-ceo-dave-girouard/, accessed Nov. 19, 2020.

225 Lazzarato, *Making of the Indebted Man*; Lazzarato, *Governing by Debt*.

226 Tanner, *Christianity and the New Spirit of Capitalism*.

as these: on one hand, such borrowers now have access to credit that allows lifestyles otherwise out of reach; on the other, such borrowers face new perils of indebtedness and obligation should society continue to make it difficult for them to access future capital to repay. Just as the microcredit industry, once hailed for helping the poor of developing countries, has come under intense fire for leading to further debt entrapment for many impoverished borrowers, these initiatives targeting needy borrowers in the developed world may face similar ethical rebukes.

Perhaps the industry most affected by digitization and certainly one of the most economically impactful is the foreign currency exchange (forex) market. With daily trade totals in the multitrillions, it dwarfs the stock market and all other markets in terms of the value exchanged. This market emerged in the 1970s after the end of the Bretton Woods settlement (1944–1971), which had sought to peg national currencies to the gold standard in an effort at post-war stabilization. Since this proved ineffectual, the gold standard was removed and national currencies were allowed to "float" in relation to one another based on values determined in a massive international currency market. Banks and currency trading firms exchange millions to billions of dollars in currency daily and take advantage of small price differentials that generate large profits at scale.

While the model is based on the millennia-old role of the moneychanger, digitization and global networks open up new pathways of connectivity and exchange, rendering larger profits.[227] These exchange networks also have massive global impact: from the perspective of governance, the market is aimed to rein in profligate nations who might devalue their currency to cover debts owed to other nations, since this would result in further devaluation from sell-offs in forex markets. Such enforced fiscal discipline hopes to enlist market dynamics to provide stability where the gold standard failed. The system has indeed fostered a kind of stability while also fixing a hierarchy of national currencies and disproportionality penalizing countries with weaker currencies. A tiered global system clearly exists and downward selling spirals have occurred where emerging markets and less solvent nations are punished.[228]

227 See, e.g., Karin Knorr Cetina and Urs Bruegger, "Traders' Engagement With Markets: A Postsocial Relationship," *Theory, Culture, and Society* 19, no. 5/6 (2002); Karin Knorr Cetina and Urs Bruegger, "Global Microstructures: The Virtual Societies of Financial Markets," *American Journal of Sociology* 107 (2002); Karin Knorr Cetina, "From Pipes to Scopes: The Flow Architecture of Financial Markets," *Distinktion. Special Issue on Economic Sociology* 7 (2003).

228 Jonathan Kirshner, *Currency and Coercion: The Political Economy of International Monetary Power* (Princeton, NJ: Princeton University Press, 1995).

What also seems novel is the unification of commodification and financialization in such markets. Philosophically this is interesting and worth further reflection. Theorists led by Marx's reflections on commodity fetishism in *Capital* volume 1 have focused on commodification as a central process to analyze when assessing the impact of capitalism. Other theorists influenced by Max Weber and Georg Simmel, among others, emphasize the necessity of understanding money and financialization as driving processes in capitalism.[229] And certainly both strands have merged in the Marxian analysis of finance capitalism as late-stage capitalism, following Rudolph Hilferding and Giovanni Arrighi, among others.[230] What forex markets present is a clear merger of these two impulses in capitalism: money as commodity; commodity as money. Money does not stand in for anything else as it typically does in the market. Money is exchanged for money and financial profit is made off money as such. The value of money is determined in relation to money. Pure exchange values are simply exchanged. When digitization is added to this self-referentiality it is difficult not to glimpse in this nexus an uncanny manifestation of the conceptual and linguistic problem of the "endless chain of signifiers" explored by poststructuralist theorists.[231] As something like a pure form, an extreme case of reification and abstraction, forex markets remain a critical site of reflection on understanding the nature of both commodification and financialization as well as their dual systemic, ethical, and conceptual impact.

Cryptocurrencies mark a departure from the world of digital currencies due both to the media involved as well as the nature of money in play. Such currencies – Bitcoin being the most well known – emerged with the creation of blockchain technology and so represent a significant iteration in digital code.[232] Essentially, blockchain is a form of networked code that requires verification of transactions from multiple nodes within a network. Computers that function as servers participate in a broad-based web of real-time transaction recording. The idea is that the public and diffuse nature of such attestations provides a trustworthy source of legitimation to confirm transactions.

229 Weber, *Economy and Society*; Georg Simmel, *The Philosophy of Money* (London: Routledge, 1978).

230 Rudolf Hilferding, *Finance Capital: A Study of the Latest Phase of Capitalist Development*, ed. T. B. Bottomore, trans. Morris Watnick and Sam Gordon (London: Routledge & Kegan Paul, 1981); Giovanni Arrighi, *The Long Twentieth Century: Money, Power, and the Origins of Our Times* (London: Verso, 1994); Ben Fine and Costas Lapavitsas, "Markets and Money in Social Theory: What Role for Economics?," *Economy and Society* 29, no. 3 (2000).

231 Jean Baudrillard, *For a Critique of the Political Economy of the Sign* (St. Louis, MO: Telos Press, 1981); Jean Baudrillard, *Simulacra and Simulation* (Ann Arbor: University of Michigan Press, 1994).

232 Satoshi Nakamoto, "Bitcoin: A Peer-to-Peer Electronic Cash System," 2009, https://bitcoin.org/bitcoin.pdf.

Rather than basing the authority of the transaction in a sovereign nation's ability to prove its currency is legitimate and so guarantee exchange, the chain of exchanges in a cryptocurrency market are confirmed via hundreds of computer "witnesses" that cannot possibly (so claim programmers) be falsified or circumvented. Coins originate in the market after a process of "mining," where computers solve a complex series of problems, undertaking a kind of electronic labor, that will eventually render them one coin. The coin can then circulate in this network of blockchain-based exchanges to be used to purchase goods or services through interfaces that accept such currency.

Thus major innovations are seen in a public and globally networked system of code that allows the verification of transactions, as well as a currency based outside the nation state that purportedly does not require the guarantee or backing of sovereignty. The basis of trust is not the authority of a nation to guarantee its currency but the confidence in the code to accurately represent the value and authenticity of the token.[233] Proponents of cryptocurrencies hail this as a breakthrough because it supposedly allows for the formation of economic communities around trust in an alternative source of authority than the nation state. Both libertarians and anarchists, while at opposite ends of the political spectrum, may see in cryptocurrencies a basis for communal transactions that circumvent state oversight and control. While nation states have assiduously sought to tax and regulate cryptocurrency markets, theoretically, at least, such markets do not require states to function.[234]

Of course, almost immediately, we can see problems with such claims of radical independence, particularly when we think about the material bases of these networks. These networks rely on physical connections between computers that are themselves located in social and political time and space, and travel on fiber optic networks that are themselves subject to federal, state, and local laws and regulations. Such computers also require electronic resources drawn from the grids and power sources that are typically regulated. In fact, one grave concern raised by critics of cryptocurrencies is the tremendous environmental impact due to the substantial amounts of energy required to mine tokens. Massive server farms exist that leave a profound ecological footprint, with some farms rivalling the electricity usage of entire nations.

---

233 Nigel Dodd, "The Social Life of Bitcoin," *Theory, Culture & Society* 35, no. 3 (2018); Philipp Hacker et al., *Regulating Blockchain: Techno-Social and Legal Challenges* (Oxford: Oxford University Press, 2019); Henrik Karlstrøm, "Do Libertarians Dream of Electric Coins? The Material Embeddedness of Bitcoin," *Distinktion: Journal of Social Theory* 15, no. 1 (2014).

234 Noteworthy is the recent merger of cryptocurrencies with sovereign monetary zones, such as the move by El Salvador to issue cryptocurrency in place of a fiat currency. The implications of this innovation (or regression) remain to be seen.

Thus far, a completely alternative crypto-based economy has not arisen, meaning that for these tokens to be meaningful and actually acquire goods, they need to be translated into values based on sovereign denominations. Bitcoins matter at the moment because of how much they are worth in dollars, for instance, not because of how much they are worth in Bitcoin. As such, these networks are parasitic on sovereign exchange networks. Much like libertarians who rely on the tax money of their neighbors to service roads or provide subvention to local telecom services, while proclaiming their radical independence and lack of need for government, hailing cryptocurrency as a radical alternative to current money systems appears disingenuous. Much remains to be seen about the potential for such connections and markets to function in the absence of nation states and the state currencies that enable most exchanges to happen.

Christian thought can reflect on any number of themes raised by cryptocurrencies. Ethical and epistemological judgments can be made about the implications of placing communal trust in a network of computer nodes. From a humanistic perspective, which would presumably prioritize human relationships and communities, trusting in the infallibility of code and the brute recording power of computers is not an obvious improvement on relying on the authority structures of the state. While this might appear to be an escape from the monopoly on violence of the state that is used to enforce that trust, it is not clear that a computer network escapes such circuits of legality and policing ultimately either. If anything, the network is one more buffering system for trust that is still based, ultimately, on state enforcement. Theological and ethical reflection might also weigh in on the merits and perils of pursuing non-state forms of association for which many cryptocurrency communities hope. Typically one's judgment on such endeavors reflects one's politics: further right and further left positions hail such manifestations optimistically while centrist and moderate positions remain closer to the machine of the state and its perceived benefits.

Conclusion

The above areas are but a small subset of a vast set of possible themes to examine. They can be further delineated and contain various subfields for inquiry. Both Christian thought and economy are capacious concepts and, depending upon how one defines the terms, any variety of objects, practices, and themes might fall under analysis. Traditional theological loci such as God, the Trinity, the incarnation, or ecclesiology, for instance, might be analyzed for economic themes, impact, and internal dynamics. A host of social issues and practices might also be examined for economic elements and their relation to Christian thought. Ecological issues are increasingly urgent given the coming environmental apocalypse and imminent collapse of the anthropocene. Such concerns almost always interact with economic practices and therefore represent an urgent site of reflection. The nature and future of work and labor are receiving much attention, particularly in light of dramatic transformations in late capitalism now exacerbated by a global pandemic and the needs of an increasingly technologically mediated society. As the shape of work shifts and labor relations continue to change with increased automatization and the introduction of AI, new ethical, theological, and philosophical concerns emerge. The pandemic is currently exacerbating a host of social inequities and highlighting the need for care economies and for equitable healthcare, in particular. Mass incarceration and the prison-industrial complex represent pressing challenges globally and in America specifically. Highlighting the racialized, economic, and debt-based nature of such practices, in tandem with labor exploitation, calls for further Christian reflection on prison abolition. The world systems' nature of economic flows means that further inquiries into decolonization and concerns of the global South are needed, and that issues pertaining to the US and Europe must be located in a global frame and situated in conversation with a much larger set of perspectives. Studies that define and clarify their terms and delineate what aspects of Christian thought and what elements of economy are under consideration will contribute much to this urgent and much needed dialogue between the two realms. While the relation is millennia old, the implications of the link between economy and Christian thought are ever present and require our best efforts at analysis and response.

Bibliography

Agamben, Giorgio. *Die Beamten des Himmels: Über Engel.* Translated by Andreas Hiepko. Berlin: Verlag der Weltreligionen im Insel Verlag, 2007.

Agamben, Giorgio. *The Kingdom and the Glory: For a Theological Genealogy of Economy and Government.* Translated by Lorenzo Chiesa and Matteo Mandarini. Stanford: Stanford University Press, 2011.

Aglietta, Michel. *Money: 5,000 Years of Debt and Power.* Translated by David Broder. London: Verso, 2018.

Ahn, Ilsup. *Just Debt: Theology, Ethics, and Neoliberalism.* Waco, TX: Baylor University Press, 2017.

Alonso, Antonio Eduardo. *Commodified Communion: Eucharist, Consumer Culture, and the Practice of Everyday Life*. New York: Fordham University Press, 2021.

Althaus-Reid, Marcella. *From Feminist Theology to Indecent Theology: Readings on Poverty, Sexual Identity and God*. London: SCM Press, 2004.

Althaus-Reid, Marcella. *Indecent Theology: Theological Perversions in Sex, Gender and Politics*. London: Routledge, 2000.

Althaus-Reid, Marcella. "Queering the Cross: The Politics of Redemption and the External Debt." *Feminist Theology* 15, no. 3 (2007): 289–301.

Althaus-Ried, Marcella Maria, Ivan Petrella, and Luiz Carlos Susin. *Another Possible World*. London: SCM Press, 2007.

Aquino, María Pilar. *Our Cry for Life: Feminist Theology from Latin America*. Maryknoll, NY: Orbis, 1993.

Arestis, Philip, and Malcolm C. Sawyer, eds. *A Handbook of Alternative Monetary Economics*. Cheltenham, UK: Edward Elgar, 2006.

Armstrong, Amaryah Shaye. "Christian Order and Racial Order: What Cedric Robinson Has to Teach Us Today." *The Bias Magazine* June 3(2020). https://christiansocialism.com/cedric-robinson-racial-order-christianity-socialism/.

Arrighi, Giovanni. *The Long Twentieth Century: Money, Power, and the Origins of Our Times*. London: Verso, 1994.

Auvinen, Tero. "At the Intersection of Sovereignty and Biopolitics: The Di-Polaric Spatializations of Money." *Foucault Studies* 9 (2010): 5–34.

Baptist, Edward E. *The Half Has Never Been Told: Slavery and the Making of American Capitalism*. New York: Basic Books, 2014.

Barclay, John. *Paul and the Gift*. Grand Rapids, MI: Eerdmans, 2015.

Bartel, Rebecca C. "Financializing the Soul: Christian Microfinance and Economic Missionization in Colombia." *Critical Research on Religion* 9, no. 1 (2020): 31–47.

Baudrillard, Jean. *For a Critique of the Political Economy of the Sign*. St. Louis, MO: Telos Press, 1981.

Baudrillard, Jean. *Simulacra and Simulation*. Ann Arbor: University of Michigan Press, 1994.

Bedford, Nancy. "Whatever Happened to Liberation Theology?" *The Christian Century*, Oct. 20, 1999, 996–1000.

Bell, Catherine M. *Ritual Theory, Ritual Practice*. New York, NY: Oxford University Press, 1992.

Bell, Catherine M. *Ritual: Perspectives and Dimensions*. New York: Oxford University Press, 1997.

Bell, Daniel M. *The Economy of Desire: Christianity and Capitalism in a Postmodern World*. Grand Rapids, MI: Baker Academic, 2012.

Belli, Humberto, and Ronald H. Nash. *Beyond Liberation Theology*. Grand Rapids, MI: Baker, 1992.

Benjamin, Walter. "Fragment 74: Capitalism as Religion." Translated by Chad Kautzer. In *Religion as Critique: The Frankfurt School's Critique of Religion*, edited by Eduardo Mendieta, 259–262. New York: Routledge, 2005.

Berlinski, Claire. *"There Is No alternative": Why Margaret Thatcher Matters*. New York: Basic Books, 2008.

Bevir, Mark. "The Labour Church Movement, 1891–1902." *Journal of British Studies* 38, no. 2 (1999): 217–245.

Bevir, Mark. *The Making of British Socialism*. Princeton, NJ: Princeton University Press, 2011.

Bhattacharya, Tithi. *Social Reproduction Theory: Remapping Class, Recentring Oppression*. London: Pluto Press, 2017.

Bialecki, Jon. "Between Stewardship and Sacrifice: Agency and Economy in a Southern California Charismatic Church." *Journal of the Royal Anthropological Institute* 14, no. 2 (2008): 372–390.

Biéler, André. *Calvin's Economic and Social Thought*. Translated by James Greig. Geneva: World Council of Churches, 2006.

Bielo, James S. "'The Mind of Christ': Financial Success, Born-again Personhood, and the Anthropology of Christianity." *Ethnos* 72, no. 3 (2007): 316–338.

Blanton, Thomas R. *Spiritual Economy: Gift Exchange in the Letters of Paul of Tarsus*. Synkrisis. New Haven, CT: Yale University Press, 2017.

Blanton, Thomas R., and Raymond Pickett, eds. *Paul and Economics: A Handbook*. Minneapolis: Fortress Press, 2017.

Block, Fred, and Peter Evans. "The State and the Economy." In *The Handbook of Economic Sociology*, edited by Neil J. Smelser and Richard Swedberg, 505–26. Princeton, NJ: Princeton University Press, 2005.

Block, Fred L., and Margaret R. Somers. *The Power of Market Fundamentalism: Karl Polanyi's Critique*. Cambridge, MA: Harvard University Press, 2014.

Blomberg, Craig L. *Neither Poverty nor Riches: A Biblical Theology of Material Possessions*. Grand Rapids: Eerdmans, 1999.

Boer, Roland. "Biting the Poor: On the Differences between Credit and Debt in Ancient Israel and Southwest Asia." *Journal of Religion and Society* 16 (2014): 1–21.

Boer, Roland. "Reconsidering Debt Remission in Light of the Ancient World." *Continental Thought and Theory* 1, no. 2 (2017): 293–305.

Boer, Roland. *The Sacred Economy of Ancient Israel*. Library of Ancient Israel. Louisville, KY: Westminster John Knox Press, 2015.

Boff, Leonardo. *Francis of Assisi: A Model for Human Liberation*. Maryknoll, NY: Orbis, 2006.

Boff, Leonardo, and Clodovis Boff. *Introducing Liberation Theology*. Translated by Paul Burns. Maryknoll, NY: Orbis, 1987.

Boltanski, Luc, and Eve Chiapello. *The New Spirit of Capitalism*. Updated ed. London: Verso, 2018.

Bourdieu, Pierre. *The Logic of Practice*. Stanford: Stanford University Press, 1990.

Bouwsma, William J. *John Calvin: A Sixteenth-Century Portrait*. New York: Oxford University Press, 1988.

Bray, Karen. *Grave Attending: A Political Theology for the Unredeemed*. New York: Fordham University Press, 2020.

Bray, Karen, and Stephen D. Moore, eds. *Religion, Emotion, Sensation: Affect Theories and Theologies*, Transdisciplinary Theological Colloquia. New York: Fordham University Press, 2019.

Bretherton, Luke. "Anglican Political Theology." In *The Wiley Blackwell Companion to Political Theology*, edited by William T. Cavanaugh and Peter Scott, 164–177. Hoboken, NJ: John Wiley & Sons, 2018.

Bretherton, Luke. *Christ and the Common Life: Political Theology and the Case for Democracy*. Grand Rapids, MI: Eerdmans, 2019.

Bretherton, Luke. "'Love Your Enemies': Usury, Citizenship, and the Friend-Enemy Distinction." *Modern Theology* 27, no. 3 (2011): 366–94.

Bretherton, Luke. *Resurrecting Democracy: Faith, Citizenship, and the Politics of a Common Life*. New York: Cambridge University Press, 2015.

Bretherton, Luke, and Devin Singh. "The Axes of Debt: A Preface to Three Essays." *Journal of Religious Ethics* 46, no. 2 (2018): 207–216.

Brown, Delwin, Sheila Greeve Davaney, and Kathryn Tanner. *Converging on Culture: Theologians in Dialogue with Cultural Analysis and Criticism*. New York: Oxford University Press, 2001.

Brown, Norman Oliver. *Life Against Death: The Psychoanalytical Meaning of History*. London: Routledge, 1959.

Brown, Peter. *Poverty and Leadership in the Later Roman Empire*. The Menahem Stern Jerusalem Lectures. Hanover, NH: University Press of New England, 2002.

Brown, Peter. *Through the Eye of a Needle: Wealth, the Fall of Rome, and the Making of Christianity in the West, 350–550 AD*. Princeton, NJ: Princeton University Press, 2012.

Brown, Wendy. *Undoing the Demos: Neoliberalism's Stealth Revolution*. New York: Zone Books, 2015.

Burchell, Graham, Colin Gordon, and Peter Miller, eds. *The Foucault Effect: Studies in Governmentality*. Chicago: University of Chicago Press, 1991.

Cahill, Lisa Sowle. *Global Justice, Christology and Christian Ethics*. New York: Cambridge University Press, 2013.

Capener, Sean. "The Price of Charity: Christian Love and Financial Anxieties." *Journal of Religious Ethics* 46, no. 2 (2018): 217–238.

Capener, Sean. "The Time That Belongs to God: The Christian Prohibition on Usury in the 12th–13th Centuries and the Making of the Subject of Debt." Ph.D. Dissertation, University of Toronto, 2021.

Capener, Sean. "When is Analogy More than a Metaphor?" *Syndicate* (February 3, 2020). https://syndicate.network/symposia/theology/divine-currency/.

Caputo, John D., and Michael J. Scanlon. *God, the Gift, and Postmodernism*. Bloomington: Indiana University Press, 1999.

Carrier, James G., ed. *A Handbook of Economic Anthropology*. Cheltham, UK: Edward Elgar, 2004.

Carter, J. Kameron. *Race: A Theological Account*. New York: Oxford University Press, 2008.

Case, Anne, and Angus Deaton. *Deaths of Despair and the Future of Capitalism*. Princeton: Princeton University Press, 2020.

Cavanaugh, William T. *Being Consumed: Economics and Christian Desire*. Grand Rapids, MI: Eerdmans, 2008.

Chakrabarty, Dipesh. *Provincializing Europe: Postcolonial Thought and Historical Difference*. Princeton, NJ: Princeton University Press, 2000.

Chilton, David. *Productive Christians in an Age of Guilt-Manipulators: A Biblical Response to Ronald J. Sider.* 3rd ed. Tyler, TX: Institute for Christian Economics, 1985.

Chirichigno, Gregory. *Debt-Slavery in Israel and the Ancient Near East*. Sheffield, UK: JSOT Press, 1993.

Choi, Jin Young, and Joerg Rieger, eds. *Faith, Class, and Labor: Intersectional Approaches in a Global Context*. Eugene, OR: Pickwick, 2020.

Chomsky, Noam. "Plutonomy and the Precariat: On the History of the U.S. Economy in Decline." *The Huffington Post*, May 8, 2012.

Christiaens, Tim. "Hayek's Vicarious Secularization of Providential Theology." *Philosophy & Social Criticism* 45, no. 1 (2019): 71–95.

Chung, Paul S., Ulrich Duchrow, and Craig L. Nessan. *Liberating Lutheran Theology: Freedom for Justice and Solidarity with Others in a Global Context*. Minneapolis, MN: Fortress Press, 2011.

Clifton, Shane. "Pentecostal Approaches to Economics." In *The Oxford Handbook of Christianity and Economics*, edited by Paul Oslington, 263–81. New York: Oxford University Press, 2014.

Cloutier, David M. *The Vice of Luxury: Economic Excess in a Consumer Age*. Washington, DC: Georgetown University Press, 2015.

Coleman, Charly. *The Spirit of French Capitalism: Economic Theology in the Age of Enlightenment*. Stanford: Stanford University Press, 2021.

Coleman, James. "The Rational Reconstruction of Society: 1992 Presidential Address." *American Sociological Review* 58, no. 1 (1993): 1–15.

Coleman, Simon. *The Globalisation of Charismatic Christianity: Spreading the Gospel of Prosperity*. Cambridge: Cambridge University Press, 2000.

Coleman, Simon, and John Eade. "Pilgrimage and Political Economy: Introduction to a Research Agenda." In *Pilgrimage and Political Economy: Translating the Sacred*, edited by Simon Coleman and John Eade, 1–20. New York: Berghahn Books, 2018.

Comaroff, Jean, and John Comaroff. "Millennial Capitalism: First Thoughts on a Second Coming." *Public Culture* 12, no. 2 (2000): 291–343.

Connolly, William E. *Capitalism and Christianity, American Style*. Durham, NC: Duke University Press, 2008.

Connolly, William E. *The Fragility of Things: Self-Organizing Processes, Neoliberal Fantasies, and Democratic Activism*. Durham, NC: Duke University Press, 2013.

Cooper, Melinda. *Family Values: Between Neoliberalism and the New Social Conservatism*. New York: Zone Books, 2017.

Cox, Harvey. *The Market as God*. Cambridge, MA: Harvard University Press, 2016.

Craig, Eleanor. "We Have Never Been Human/e: The Laws of Burgos and the Philosophy of Coloniality in the Americas." In *Beyond Man: Race, Coloniality, and Philosophy of Religion*, edited by Yountae An and Eleanor Craig, 86–107. Durham, NC: Duke University Press, 2021.

Curran, Charles E. "Catholic Social Teaching." *The Good Society* 10, no. 1 (2001): 1–6.

Dane, Perry. "Corporations." In *The Routledge Handbook of Economic Theology*, edited by Stefan Schwarzkopf, 144–53. London: Routledge, 2020.

Dardot, Pierre, and Christian Laval. *Common: On Revolution in the 21st Century*. London: Bloomsbury, 2019.

Davis, Natalie Zemon. *The Gift in Sixteenth-Century France*. Madison: University of Wisconsin Press, 2000.

Day, Keri. *Religious Resistance to Neoliberalism: Womanist and Black Feminist Perspectives*. New York: Palgrave Macmillan, 2016.

Day, Keri. "We Need a Pentecost." *The Christian Century*, May 3 2018, https://www.christiancentury.org/article/critical-essay/we-need-pentecost.

De Gruchy, John W. *Liberating Reformed Theology: A South African Contribution to an Ecumenical Debate*. Grand Rapids, MI: Eerdmans, 1991.

Dean, Mitchell. *Governmentality: Power and Rule in Modern Society*. 2nd ed. London: SAGE, 2010.

Deaton, Angus. *The Great Escape: Health, Wealth, and the Origins of Inequality*. Princeton, NJ: Princeton University Press, 2013.

DeBerri, Edward, James Hug, and Peter Henriot. *Catholic Social Teaching: Our Best Kept Secret*. 4th ed. New York: Orbis, 2003.

Deleuze, Gilles, and Félix Guattari. *Anti-Oedipus: Capitalism and Schizophrenia*. Minneapolis: University of Minnesota Press, 1983.

Dienst, Richard. *The Bonds of Debt*. London: Verso, 2011.

Dodd, Nigel. "The Social Life of Bitcoin." *Theory, Culture & Society* 35, no. 3 (2018): 35–56.

Dodd, Nigel. *The Social Life of Money*. Princeton, NJ: Princeton University Press, 2014.

Dommen, Edward, and James D. Bratt, eds. *John Calvin Rediscovered: The Impact of His Social and Economic Thought*. Louisville, KY: Westminster John Knox Press, 2007.

Dorrien, Gary. "Economic Democracy as Political Theology: The British Anglican Socialist Tradition." *Anglican Theological Review* 102, no. 4 (2020): 539–573.

Douglas, Alexander. *The Philosophy of Debt*. London: Routledge, 2016.

Duchrow, Ulrich. *Alternatives to Global Capitalism: Drawn from Biblical History, Designed for Political Action*. Heidelberg: International Books: Kairos Europa, 1995.

Dussel, Enrique. *Las metáforas teológicas de Marx*. Estella: Editorial Verbo Divino, 1993.

Dussel, Enrique. *Towards an Unknown Marx: A Commentary on the Manuscripts of 1861–63*. Translated by Yolanda Angulo. London: Routledge, 2001.

Eaton, David H. "The Economists of the Reformation: An Overview of Reformation Teaching Concerning Work, Wealth, and Interest." *SAGE Open* 3, no. 3 (2013): 1–9.

Ekelund Jr., Robert B., Robert F. Hébert, and Robert D. Tollison. "The Political Economy of the Medieval Church." In *The Oxford Handbook of the Economics of Religion*, edited by Rachel M. McCleary, 305–22. Oxford: Oxford University Press, 2011.

Ellacuría, Ignacio, and Jon Sobrino. *Mysterium Liberationis: Fundamental Concepts of Liberation Theology*. Maryknoll, NY: Orbis, 1993.

Ellerman, David. "The Democratic Firm: An Argument Based on Ordinary Jurisprudence." *Journal of Business Ethics* 21, no. 2 (1999): 111–124.

Esposito, Roberto. *Two: The Machine of Political Theology and the Place of Thought*. Translated by Zakiya Hanafi. New York: Fordham University Press, 2015.

Federici, Silvia. *Caliban and the Witch: Women, the Body, and Primitive Accumulation*. Brooklyn, NY: Autonomedia, 2004.

Federici, Silvia. *Wages Against Housework*. Bristol, UK: Falling Wall Press and the Power of Women Collective, 1975.

Fine, Ben, and Costas Lapavitsas. "Markets and Money in Social Theory: What Role for Economics?". *Economy and Society* 29, no. 3 (2000): 357–382.

Flannery, Kent V., and Joyce Marcus. *The Creation of Inequality: How our Prehistoric Ancestors set the Stage for Monarchy, Slavery, and Empire*. Cambridge, MA: Harvard University Press, 2012.

Foucault, Michel. *Archaeology of Knowledge*. London: Routledge, 2002.

Foucault, Michel. *Discipline and Punish: The Birth of the Prison*. 2nd ed. New York: Vintage Books, 1995.

Foucault, Michel. *Security, Territory, Population: Lectures at the Collège de France, 1977–1978*. Edited by Michel Senellart and Arnold I. Davidson. New York: Palgrave Macmillan, 2007.

Foucault, Michel. *Society Must Be Defended: Lectures at the Collège de France, 1975–76*. Edited by Mauro Bertani, Alessandro Fontana, François Ewald and David Macey. New York: Picador, 2003.

Fraser, Nancy. "Contradictions of Capital and Care." *New Left Review* 100 (2016): 99–117.

Fraser, Nancy. "Expropriation and Exploitation in Racialized Capitalism: A Reply to Michael Dawson." *Critical Historical Studies* 3, no. 1 (Spring 2016): 163–178.

Freudenberg, Matthias. "Economic and Social Ethics in the Work of John Calvin." *HTS: Theological Studies* 65, no. 1 (2009): 634–40.

Friedman, Benjamin M. *Religion and the Rise of Capitalism*. New York: Alfred A. Knopf, 2021.

Friedman, Thomas. *The Lexus and the Olive Tree*. New York: Anchor Books, 2000.

Fukuyama, Francis. *The End of History and the Last Man*. New York: Free Press, 1992.

Funkenstein, Amos. *Theology and the Scientific Imagination from the Middle Ages to the Seventeenth Century*. Princeton, NJ: Princeton University Press, 1986.

Galeano, Eduardo. *Open Veins of Latin America: Five Centuries of the Pillage of a Continent*. 25th anniversary ed. New York: Monthly Review Press, 1997.

Gierke, Otto. *Political Theories of the Middle Age*. Translated by Frederic William Maitland. Cambridge: Cambridge University Press, 1900.

Gilligan, Carol. *In a Different Voice: Psychological Theory and Women's Development*. New ed. Cambridge, MA: Harvard University Press, 1993.

González, George J. *Shape-Shifting Capital: Spiritual Management, Critical Theory, and the Ethnographic Project*. Lanham, MD: Lexington Books, 2015.

Goodchild, Philip. *Credit and Faith*. Lanham, MD: Rowman & Littlefield, 2020.

Goodchild, Philip. *Economic Theology: Credit and Faith II*. Lanham, MD: Rowman & Littlefield, 2020.

Goodchild, Philip. *The Metaphysics of Trust: Credit and Faith III*. Lanham, MD: Rowman & Littlefield, 2021.

Goodchild, Philip. *Theology of Money*. Durham, NC: Duke University Press, 2009.

Goodhart, Charles. "The Two Concepts of Money: Implications for the Analysis of Optimal Currency Areas." *European Journal of Political Economy* 14 (1998): 407–432.

Gorski, Philip S. *The Protestant Ethic Revisited*. Philadelphia: Temple University Press, 2011.

Goux, Jean-Joseph. *The Coiners of Language*. Norman, OK: University of Oklahoma Press, 1994.

Graeber, David. *Debt: The First 5,000 Years*. Updated and Expanded ed. Brooklyn: Melville House, 2014.

Graeber, David, and David Wengrow. *The Dawn of Everything: A New History of Humanity*. New York: Farrar, Straus and Giroux, 2021.

Granovetter, Mark S. "Economic Action and Social Structure: The Problem of Embeddedness." *American Journal of Sociology* 91 (November 1985): 481–510.

Granovetter, Mark S., and Richard Swedberg. *The Sociology of Economic Life*. Boulder, CO: Westview Press, 1992.

Grau, Marion. *Of Divine Economy: Refinancing Redemption*. New York: T & T Clark International, 2004.

Green, Roger K. "Neoliberalism and Eurochristianity." *Religions* 12, no. 9 (2021): 688.

Gregory, C. A. *Gifts and Commodities*. London: Academic Press, 1982.

Grewal, David Singh. "The Political Theology of *Laissez-Faire*: From *Philia* to Self-Love in Commercial Society." *Political Theology* 17, no. 5 (2016): 417–433.

Grimes, Katie Walker. *Christ Divided: Antiblackness as Corporate Vice*. Minneapolis, MN: Fortress Press, 2017.

Gutiérrez, Gustavo. *The God of Life*. Translated by Matthew J. O'Connell. Maryknoll, NY: Orbis, 1991.

Gutiérrez, Gustavo. *A Theology of Liberation: History, Politics, and Salvation*. Translated by Sister Caridad Inda. Rev. ed. Maryknoll, NY: Orbis, 1988.

Hacker, Philipp, Ioannis Lianos, Georgios Dimitropoulos, and Stefan Eich. *Regulating Blockchain: Techno-Social and Legal Challenges*. Oxford: Oxford University Press, 2019.

Hacking, Ian. *Scientific Revolutions*. Oxford: Oxford University Press, 1981.

Hagemann, Harald, Yukihiro Ikeda, and Tamotsu Nishizawa. *Austrian Economics in Transition: From Carl Menger to Friedrich Hayek*. New York: Palgrave Macmillan, 2010.

Hagen, Jürgen von, and Michael I. Welker, eds. *Money as God? The Monetization of the Market and the Impact on Religion, Politics, Law, and Ethics*. Cambridge: Cambridge University Press, 2014.

Hall, Peter A., and David W. Soskice. *Varieties of Capitalism: The Institutional Foundations of Comparative Advantage*. New York: Oxford University Press, 2001.

Hann, C. M., and Keith Hart. *Economic Anthropology*. Cambridge: Polity, 2011.

Hart, William David. "Constellations: Capitalism, Antiblackness, Afro-Pessimism, and Black Optimism." *American Journal of Theology & Philosophy* 39, no. 1 (2018): 5–33.

Harvey, David. *The Condition of Postmodernity: An Enquiry into the Origins of Cultural Change*. Oxford: Blackwell, 1989.

Hawtrey, Kim. "Anglicanism." In *The Oxford Handbook of Christianity and Economics*, edited by Paul Oslington, 177–96. New York: Oxford University Press, 2014.

Haynes, Naomi. "On the Potential and Problems of Pentecostal Exchange." *American Anthropologist* 115, no. 1 (2013): 85–95.

Held, Virginia. *The Ethics of Care: Personal, Political, and Global*. Oxford: Oxford University Press, 2006.

Hilferding, Rudolf. *Finance Capital: A Study of the Latest Phase of Capitalist Development*. Translated by Morris Watnick and Sam Gordon. Edited by T. B. Bottomore. London: Routledge & Kegan Paul, 1981.

Hill, Emily Beth. *Marketing and Christian Proclamation in Theological Perspective*. Lanham, MD: Lexington Books/Fortress Academic, 2021.

Hill, Lisa. "The Hidden Theology of Adam Smith." *European Journal of History of Economic Thought* 8, no. 1 (2001): 1–29.

Himes, Kenneth R. "Consumerism and Christian Ethics." *Theological Studies* 68, no. 1 (2007): 132–153.

Hinson-Hasty, Elizabeth L. *The Problem of Wealth: A Christian Response to a Culture of Affluence*. Maryknoll: Orbis, 2017.

Hirschfeld, Mary L. *Aquinas and the Market: Toward a Humane Economy*. Cambridge, MA: Harvard University Press, 2018.

Hirschman, Albert. *The Passions and the Interests: Political Arguments for Capitalism Before its Triumph*. Princeton, NJ: Princeton University Press, 1977.

Hirschman, Albert. "Rival Interpretations of Market Society: Civilizing, Destructive, or Feeble?". *Journal of Economic Literature* 20 (1982): 1463–1484.

Ho, Karen Z. *Liquidated: An Ethnography of Wall Street*. Durham, NC: Duke University Press, 2009.

Ho, Karen Z. "Situating Global Capitalisms: A View From Wall Street Investment Banks." *Cultural Anthropology* 20, no. 1 (2005): 68–96.

Hoogvelt, Ankie. *Globalization and the Postcolonial World: The New Political Economy of Development*. 2nd ed. Baltimore, MD: Johns Hopkins University Press, 2001.

Hudson, Michael. "The Archaeology of Money: Debt versus Barter Theories of Money's Origins." Chap. 5 In *Credit and State Theories of Money: The Contributions of A. Mitchell Innes*, edited by L. Randall Wray, 99–127. Northampton, MA: Edward Elgar, 2004.

Hudson, Michael, and Marc Van de Mieroop, eds. *Debt and Economic Renewal in the Ancient Near East*. Bethesda, MD: CDL Press, 2002.

Hudson, Michael, and Cornelia Wunsch, eds. *Creating Economic Order: Record-Keeping, Standardization, and the Development of Accounting in the Ancient Near East*. Bethesda, MD: CDL Press, 2004.

Humphrey, Caroline, and Stephen Hugh-Jones. *Barter, Exchange, and Value: An Anthropological Approach*. Cambridge: Cambridge University Press, 1992.

Hus, Jan. *The Letters of John Hus*. London: Hodder and Stoughton, 1904.

Iannaccone, Laurence, and William S. Bainbridge. "Economics of Religion." In *The Routledge Companion to the Study of Religion*, edited by John Hinnells, 461–475. London: Routledge, 2010.

Ibarra, Herminia, and Morten T. Hansen. "Are You a Collaborative Leader?" *Harvard Business Review*, July-August 2011, https://hbr.org/2011/07/are-you-a-collaborative-leader.

Ingham, Geoffrey K. *Capitalism*. Cambridge: Polity, 2008.

Ingham, Geoffrey K. *The Nature of Money*. Cambridge: Polity, 2004.

Ingham, Geoffrey K. "On the Underdevelopment of the 'Sociology of Money'." *Acta Sociologica* 41, no. 1 (1998): 3–18.

Innes, A. Mitchell. "The Credit Theory of Money." *The Banking Law Journal* (1914): 151–168.

Innes, A. Mitchell. "What Is Money?". *The Banking Law Journal* (1913): 377–408.

James, C. L. R. *The Black Jacobins: Toussaint l'Ouverture and the San Domingo Revolution*. 2nd ed. New York: Vintage Books, 1963.

Jennings, Willie James. *The Christian Imagination: Theology and the Origins of Race.* New Haven, CT: Yale University Press, 2010.

Jones, Laurie Beth. *Jesus, CEO: Using Ancient Wisdom for Visionary Leadership.* 25th Anniv. ed. New York: Hachette Go, 2021.

Joseph, Miranda. *Debt to Society: Accounting for Life Under Capitalism.* Minneapolis: University of Minnesota Press, 2014.

Kantorowicz, Ernst. *The King's Two Bodies: A Study in Medieval Political Theology.* Princeton, NJ: Princeton University Press, 1957.

Karlstrøm, Henrik. "Do Libertarians Dream of Electric Coins? The Material Embeddedness of Bitcoin." *Distinktion: Journal of Social Theory* 15, no. 1 (2014): 23–36.

Keel, Terence. *Divine Variations: How Christian Thought Became Racial Science.* Stanford: Stanford University Press, 2018.

Keynes, John Maynard. *The General Theory of Employment, Interest, and Money.* New York: Harcourt, Brace, 1936.

Kim, Sebastian C. H. *Theology in the Public Sphere.* London: SCM Press, 2011.

Kirby, Benjamin. "Pentecostalism, Economics, Capitalism: Putting the Protestant Ethic to Work." *Religion* 49, no. 4 (2019): 571–591.

Kirkland, Scott A. "Hayekian Neoliberalism as Negative Political Theology." *Political Theology* 21, no. 7 (2020): 623–633.

Kirshner, Jonathan. *Currency and Coercion: The Political Economy of International Monetary Power.* Princeton, NJ: Princeton University Press, 1995.

Kirwan, Michael. *Political Theology: A New Introduction.* London: Darton Longman & Todd, 2008.

Knapp, Georg Friedrich. *The State Theory of Money.* Edited by H. M. Lucas and James Bonar. Abridged ed. London: Macmillan, 1924.

Knodel, Jamie. "Texas Lt. Gov. Dan Patrick Suggests He, Other Seniors Willing to Die to Get Economy Going Again." *NBC News*, Mar 24, 2020, https://www.nbcnews.com/news/us-news/texas-lt-gov-dan-patrick-suggests-he-other-seniors-willing-n1167341.

Knorr Cetina, Karin. "From Pipes to Scopes: The Flow Architecture of Financial Markets." *Distinktion. Special Issue on Economic Sociology* 7 (2003): 7–23.

Knorr Cetina, Karin, and Urs Bruegger. "Global Microstructures: The Virtual Societies of Financial Markets." *American Journal of Sociology* 107 (2002): 905–50.

Knorr Cetina, Karin, and Urs Bruegger. "Traders' Engagement With Markets: A Postsocial Relationship." *Theory, Culture, and Society* 19, no. 5/6 (2002): 161–185.

Koessler, Maximilian. "The Person in Imagination or Persona Ficta of the Corporation." *Louisiana Law Review* 9, no. 4 (1949): 435–449.

Konings, Martijn. *Capital and Time: For a New Critique of Neoliberal Reason.* Stanford: Stanford University Press, 2018.

Koopman, Nico. "Theology and the Fulfillment of Social and Economic Rights." In *Theories of Social and Economic Justice*, edited by A. van der Walt. Stellenbosch: Sunmedia, 2005.

Kotsko, Adam. *Neoliberalism's Demons: On the Political Theology of Late Capital.* Stanford: Stanford University Press, 2018.

Kotsko, Adam. *The Prince of This World.* Stanford: Stanford University Press, 2016.

Kruse, Kevin Michael. *One Nation under God: How Corporate America Invented Christian America.* New York: Basic Books, 2015.

Langholm, Odd. *Economics in the Medieval Schools: Wealth, Exchange, Value, Money and Usury according to the Paris Theological Tradition, 1200–1350* Leiden: Brill, 1992.

Langholm, Odd. *The Merchant in the Confessional: Trade and Price in the Pre-Reformation Penitential Handbooks.* Leiden: Brill, 2003.

Lazzarato, Maurizio. *Governing by Debt.* Translated by Joshua David Jordan. Cambridge, MA: Semiotext(e); MIT Press, 2015.

Lazzarato, Maurizio. *The Making of the Indebted Man: An Essay on the Neoliberal Condition.* Translated by Joshua David Jordan. Los Angeles: Semiotext(e), 2012.

Le Goff, Jacques. *Money and the Middle Ages: An Essay in Historical Anthropology.* [in Text in English; translated from French.] Cambridge: Polity, 2012.

Le Goff, Jacques. *Your Money or Your Life: Economy and Religion in the Middle Ages.* Translated by Patricia Ranum. New York: Zone Books, 1998.

Lebner, Ashley. *Redescribing Relations: Strathernian Conversations on Ethnography, Knowledge and Politics.* New York: Berghahn Books, 2017.

Lee, Benjamin, and Edward LiPuma. *Financial Derivatives and the Globalization of Risk.* Durham, NC: Duke University Press, 2004.

Lee, Frederic S. "Heterodox Economics." In *The New Palgrave Dictionary of Economics*, edited by Steven N. Durlauf and Lawrence E. Blume. New York: Palgrave Macmillan, 2008.

Leonard, Thomas C. "Religion and Evolution in Progressive Era Political Economy: Adversaries or Allies?". *History of Political Economy* 43, no. 3 (2011): 429–469.

Leong, Nancy. "Racial Capitalism." *Harvard Law Review* 126, no. 8 (2013): 2151–2226.

Leshem, Dotan. *The Origins of Neoliberalism: Modeling the Economy from Jesus to Foucault.* New York: Columbia University Press, 2016.

Lindberg, Carter, and Paul Wee. *The Forgotten Luther: Reclaiming the Social-Economic Dimension of the Reformation.* Minneapolis: Lutheran University Press, 2016.

Lofton, Kathryn. *Consuming Religion.* Chicago: University of Chicago Press, 2017.

Long, D. Stephen. *Divine Economy: Theology and the Market.* London: Routledge, 2000.

Long, D. Stephen, Nancy Ruth Fox, and Tripp York. *Calculated Futures: Theology, Ethics, and Economics.* Waco, TX: Baylor University Press, 2007.

Longenecker, Bruce W., and Kelly D. Liebengood, eds. *Engaging Economics: New Testament Scenarios and Early Christian Reception.* Grand Rapids, MI: Eerdmans, 2009.

LoRusso, James Dennis. *Spirituality, Corporate Culture, and American Business: The Neoliberal Ethic and the Spirit of Global Capital.* New York: Bloomsbury Academic, 2017.

MacDonald, James. *A Free Nation Deep in Debt: The Financial Roots of Democracy.* New York: Farrar, Straus and Giroux, 2003.

Mandeville, Bernard. *The Fable of the Bees: Or, Private Vices and Public Benefits.* Oxford: Clarendon, 1924.

Marçal, Katrine. *Who Cooked Adam Smith's Dinner? A Story about Women and Economics.* Translated by Saskia Vogel. London: Portobello Books, 2015.

Marion, Jean-Luc. *Being Given: Toward a Phenomenology of Givenness.* Stanford: Stanford University Press, 2002.

Martin, Randy. *Financialization of Daily Life.* Philadelphia: Temple University Press, 2002.

Marx, Karl. *Capital: A Critique of Political Economy.* Translated by Ben Fowkes. Vol. 1, London: Penguin Books, 1976.

Masuzawa, Tomoko. *In Search of Dreamtime: The Quest for the Origin of Religion.* Chicago: University of Chicago Press, 1993.

Masuzawa, Tomoko. *The Invention of World Religions, or, How European Universalism Was Preserved in the Language of Pluralism.* Chicago: University of Chicago Press, 2005.

Maurer, Bill. "Repressed Futures: Financial Derivatives' Theological Unconscious." *Economy and Society* 31, no. 1 (2002): 15–36.

Maxwell, John C. *The 21 Irrefutable Laws of Leadership: Follow Them and People will Follow You.* Rev. and updated 10th anniv. ed. Nashville, TN: Thomas Nelson, 2007.

May, Henry Farnham. *Protestant Churches and Industrial America.* New York: Harper, 1949.

McCarraher, Eugene. *The Enchantments of Mammon: How Capitalism Became the Religion of Modernity.* Cambridge, MA: The Belknap Press of Harvard University Press, 2019.

McClanahan, Annie. *Dead Pledges: Debt, Crisis, and Twenty-First-Century Culture.* Post 45. Stanford: Stanford University Press, 2017.

McCormick, John P. "Transcending Weber's Categories of Modernity? The Early Lukács and Schmitt on the Rationalization Thesis." *New German Critique* 75 (Autumn, 1998): 133–177.

McLaughlin, Levi, Aike P. Rots, Jolyon Baraka Thomas, and Chika Watanabe. "Why Scholars of Religion Must Investigate the Corporate Form." *Journal of the American Academy of Religion* 88, no. 3 (2020): 693–725.

Meeks, M. Douglas. *God the Economist: The Doctrine of God and Political Economy.* Minneapolis: Fortress Press, 1989.

Menger, Carl. "On the Origin of Money." *The Economic Journal* 2, no. 6 (1892): 239–255.

Milbank, John. "Can a Gift Be Given? Prolegomena to a Future Trinitarian Metaphysic." *Modern Theology* 11, no. 1 (January 1995): 119–161.

Milbank, John. *Theology and Social Theory: Beyond Secular Reason.* 2nd ed. Oxford: Blackwell, 2006.

Miller, Vincent. *Consuming Religion: Christian Faith and Practice in a Consumer Culture.* New York: Continuum, 2004.

Moltmann, Jürgen. *God for a Secular Society: The Public Relevance of Theology.* London: SCM Press, 1999.

Moreton, Bethany. *To Serve God and Wal-Mart: The Making of Christian Free Enterprise.* Cambridge, MA: Harvard University Press, 2009.

Morgan, Glenn. "The Theory of Comparative Capitalisms and the Possibilities for Local Variation." *European Review* 15, no. 3 (2007): 353–371.

Morgan, Kathryn A., ed. *Popular Tyranny: Sovereignty and its Discontents in Ancient Greece.* Austin: University of Texas Press, 2003.

Mott, Stephen Charles. *Biblical Ethics and Social Change.* 2nd ed. New York: Oxford University Press, 2011.

Nakamoto, Satoshi. "Bitcoin: A Peer-to-Peer Electronic Cash System." 2009, https://bitcoin.org/bitcoin.pdf.

Nelson, Julie A. "Is Economics a Natural Science?". *Social Research* 71, no. 2 (2004): 211–222.

Nelson, Robert H. *Economics as Religion: From Samuelson to Chicago and Beyond.* University Park, PA: Pennsylvania State University Press, 2001.

Nelson, Robert H. *Reaching for Heaven on Earth: The Theological Meaning of Economics.* Savage, MD: Rowman & Littlefield, 1991.

Newheiser, David. "Desacralizing Political Theology: Dionysius the Areopagite and Giorgio Agamben." *Modern Theology* 36, no. 1 (2020): 76–89.

Newheiser, David. *Hope in a Secular Age: Deconstruction, Negative Theology and the Future of Faith.* Cambridge: Cambridge University Press, 2019.

Noddings, Nel. *Caring: A Feminine Approach to Ethics & Moral Education.* 2nd ed. Berkeley: University of California Press, 2003.

Northcott, Michael. "Political Economy." In *The Wiley Blackwell Companion to Political Theology*, edited by William T. Cavanaugh and Peter Scott, 531–543. Hoboken, NJ: John Wiley & Sons, 2018.

Novak, Michael. *The Catholic Ethic and the Spirit of Capitalism.* New York: Free Press, 1993.

Oslington, Paul, ed. *Adam Smith as Theologian.* New York: Routledge, 2011.

Oslington, Paul, ed. *The Oxford Handbook of Christianity and Economics.* New York: Oxford University Press, 2014.

Oslington, Paul, ed. *Political Economy as Natural Theology: Smith, Malthus and Their Followers.* London: Routledge, 2018.

Owens, Patricia. *Economy of Force: Counterinsurgency and the Historical Rise of the Social*. Cambridge: Cambridge University Press, 2015.

Patinkin, Don, and Otto Steiger. "In Search of the 'Veil of Money' and the 'Neutrality of Money': A Note on the Origin of Terms." *Scandinavian Journal of Economics* 91, no. 1 (1989): 131–146.

Pawlikowski, John T. "Modern Catholic Teaching on the Economy: An Analysis and Evaluation." In *Christianity and Capitalism: Perspectives on Religion, Liberalism and the Economy*, edited by Bruce Grelle and David A. Krueger, 3–24. Chicago: Center for the Scientific Study of Religion, 1986.

Petrella, Ivan. *Beyond Liberation Theology: A Polemic*. London: SCM Press, 2008.

Petrella, Ivan. *The Future of Liberation Theology: An Argument and Manifesto*. Aldershot, UK: Ashgate, 2004.

Phelps, Hollis. *Jesus and the Politics of Mammon*. Critical Theory & Biblical Studies. Eugene, OR: Cascade Books, 2019.

Phelps, Hollis. "Overcoming Redemption: Neoliberalism, Atonement, and the Logic of Debt." *Political Theology* 17, no. 3 (2016): 264–282.

Phelps, Hollis. "Rethinking Debt: Theology, Indebted Subjects, and Student Loans." *Dialog: A Journal of Theology* 55, no. 1 (2016): 31–41.

Piketty, Thomas. *Capital and Ideology*. Translated by Arthur Goldhammer. Cambridge, MA: The Belknap Press of Harvard University Press, 2020.

Piketty, Thomas. *Capital in the Twenty-First Century*. Translated by Arthur Goldhammer. Cambridge, MA: The Belknap Press of Harvard University Press, 2014.

Polanyi, Karl. *The Great Transformation*. New York: Rinehart, 1944.

Polanyi, Karl. *Trade and Market in the Early Empires*. Glencoe, IL: Free Press, 1957.

Porterfield, Amanda. *Corporate Spirit: Religion and the Rise of the Modern Corporation*. Oxford: Oxford University Press, 2018.

Przywara, Erich. *Analogia Entis: Metaphysics, Original Structure and Universal Rhythm*. Translated by John Betz and David Bentley Hart. Grand Rapids, MI: Eerdmans, 2014.

Quigley, Jennifer A. *Divine Accounting: Theo-Economics in Early Christianity*. Synkrisis. New Haven, CT: Yale University Press, 2021.

Ramey, Joshua Alan. *Politics of Divination: Neoliberal Endgame and the Religion of Contingency*. Lanham, MD: Rowman & Littlefield, 2016.

Reno, R. R. "Questioning the Shutdown." *First Things*, March 20, 2020, https://www.firstthings.com/web-exclusives/2020/03/questioning-the-shutdown.

Reno, R. R. "Say 'No" to Death's Dominion." *First Things*, March 23, 2020, https://www.firstthings.com/web-exclusives/2020/03/say-no-to-deaths-dominion.

Rieger, Joerg. *No Rising Tide: Theology, Economics, and the Future*. Minneapolis, MN: Fortress Press, 2009.

Rieger, Joerg. *Opting for the Margins: Postmodernity and Liberation in Christian Theology*. New York: Oxford University Press, 2003.

Rieger, Joerg, ed. *Religion, Theology, and Class: Fresh Engagements After Long Silence*. New York: Palgrave Macmillan, 2013.

Rieger, Joerg, ed. "Rethinking Religion, Theology, and What Really Matters: The Ultimate Concerns of Essential Work." *Stellenbosch Theological Journal* 7 (2021): 1–19.

Rieger, Joerg, and Kwok Pui-Lan. *Occupy Religion: Theology of the Multitude*. Lanham, MD: Rowman & Littlefield, 2012.

Robinson, Cedric. *An Anthropology of Marxism*. New York: Ashgate, 2001.

Robinson, Cedric. *Black Marxism: The Making of the Black Radical Tradition*. Chapel Hill, NC: University of North Carolina Press, 2000.

Rose, Marika. "'It's Not the Money but the Love of Money That Is the Root of All Evil': Social Subjection, Machinic Enslavement and the Limits of Anglican Social Theology." *Religions* 7, no. 8 (2016): 50–61.

Rose, Marika. *A Theology of Failure: Žižek Against Christian Innocence*. New York: Fordham University Press, 2019.

Rosenberg, Jordana (Jordy). *Critical Enthusiasm: Capital Accumulation and the Transformation of Religious Passion*. New York: Oxford University Press, 2011.

Ruane, Paige, narrator. "Episode 13: Catholicism." Podcast audio. *Oxide Radio*. June 24, 2017. http://www.oxideradio.org/episodes/2017/6/24/episode-13-religion.

Rucker, Philip. "Mitt Romney Says 'Corporations Are People'." *Washington Post*, August 11, 2011, https://www.washingtonpost.com/politics/mitt-romney-says-corporations-are-people/2011/08/11/gIQABwZ38I_story.html.

Runions, Erin. "Carceral Sacrificonomics in the Time of Pandemic." *Critical Research on Religion* 9, no. 1 (2021): 98–102.

Runions, Erin. "Immobile Theologies, Carceral Affects: Interest and Debt in Faith-Based Prison Programs." In *Religion, Emotion, Sensation: Affect Theories and Theologies*, edited by Karen Bray and Stephen D. Moore. New York: Fordham University Press, 2019.

Sahlins, Marshall. *How "Natives" Think: About Captain Cook, for Example*. Chicago: University of Chicago Press, 1995.

Santori, Paolo. "Was Aquinas a 'Universal Economist'?". *History of Economics Review* 72, no. 1 (2019): 79–91.

Schlabach, Gerald. *And Who is My Neighbor?: Poverty, Privilege, and the Gospel of Christ*. Scottdale, PA: Herald Press, 1990.

Schwarzkopf, Stefan. "An Introduction to Economic Theology." In *The Routledge Handbook of Economic Theology*, edited by Stefan Schwarzkopf, 1–15. London: Routledge, 2020.

Schwarzkopf, Stefan. "Markets and Marketization." In *The Routledge Handbook of Economic Theology*, edited by Stefan Schwarzkopf, 163–172. London: Routledge, 2020.

Schwarzkopf, Stefan, ed. *The Routledge Handbook of Economic Theology*. London: Routledge, 2020.

Scott, James C. *Against the Grain: A Deep History of the Earliest States*. New Haven: Yale University Press, 2017.

Seaford, Richard. "Tragic Tyranny." In *Popular Tyranny: Sovereignty and its Discontents in Ancient Greece*, edited by Kathryn A. Morgan, 95–116. Austin: University of Texas Press, 2003.

Sebastian, D. F. "The Economy is a Spirit World: Spirit of Scarcity, Spirit of God." *Journal of the European Pentecostal Theological Association* 39, no. 1 (2019): 62–78.

Sekula, Allan. "The Body and Archive." *October* 39 (1986): 3–64.

Shapiro, Ian. *The Flight from Reality in the Human Sciences*. Princeton, NJ: Princeton University Press, 2005.

Shell, Marc. *The Economy of Literature*. Baltimore: Johns Hopkins University Press, 1978.

Shell, Marc. *Money, Language, and Thought: Literary and Philosophical Economies from the Medieval to the Modern Era*. Berkeley: University of California Press, 1982.

Sider, Ronald J. *Rich Christians in an Age of Hunger: A Biblical Study*. 2nd ed. Downers Grove, IL: InterVarsity Press, 1984.

Simmel, Georg. *The Philosophy of Money*. London: Routledge, 1978.

Simon, Derek. "The New Political Theology of Metz: Confronting Schmitt's Decisionist Political Theology of Exclusion." *Horizons* 30, no. 2 (2003): 227–254.

Simonsson, Ida. "The Order of Value: Christian Theology and the Market Economy." PhD Dissertation, Acta Universitatis Upsaliensis, 2021.

Singh, Devin. "COVID-19 Is Exposing Market Fundamentalism's Many Moral and Practical Flaws." *Washington Post*, April 4, 2020, https://www.washingtonpost.com/outlook/2020/04/10/covid-19-is-exposing-market-fundamentalisms-many-moral-practical-flaws/.

Singh, Devin. "Debt Cancellation as Sovereign Crisis Management." *Cosmologics*, Jan 18 2016, http://cosmologicsmagazine.com/devin-singh-debt-cancellation-as-sovereign-crisis-management/.

Singh, Devin. "Defaced Coins in a Utopian Market." *Political Theology Network Blog*, July 9, 2020, https://politicaltheology.com/defaced-coins-in-a-utopian-market/.

Singh, Devin. *Divine Currency: The Theological Power of Money in the West*. Stanford: Stanford University Press, 2018.

Singh, Devin. "Economics." In *T&T Clark Handbook of Public Theology*, edited by Christoph Hübenthal and Christiane Alpers, 414–431. New York: Bloomsbury, 2022.

Singh, Devin. "Introduction Part II: Debt, Obligation, and Care on the Commons." In *Reimagining Leadership on the Commons: Shifting the Paradigm for a More Ethical, Equitable, and Just World*, edited by Devin Singh, Randal Joy Thompson and Kathleen A. Curran, 31–55. Bingley, UK: Emerald, 2021.

Singh, Devin. "Irrational Exuberance: Hope, Expectation, and Cool Market Logic." *Political Theology* 17, no. 2 (2016): 120–136.

Singh, Devin. "Protest at the Void: Theological Challenges to Capitalist Totality." In *Religion, Protest, and Social Upheaval*, edited by Matthew T. Eggemeier, Peter Joseph Fritz and Karen V. Guth. New York: Fordham University Press, 2022.

Singh, Devin. "Religion, Economics, and the Stories We Tell." *Harvard Divinity Bulletin* Autumn/Winter (2021). https://bulletin.hds.harvard.edu/religion-economics-and-the-stories-we-tell/.

Singh, Devin. "Sovereign Debt." *Journal of Religious Ethics* 46, no. 2 (2018): 239–266.

Singh, Devin. "Until We Are One? Biopolitics and the United Body." In *'In Christ' in Paul: Explorations in Paul's Theology of Union and Participation*, edited by Kevin J. Vanhoozer, Constantine R. Campbell and Michael J. Thate. WUNT/II. Tuebingen: Mohr Siebeck, 2014.

Skidelsky, Robert, and Edward Skidelsky. *How Much Is Enough? Money and the Good Life*. New York: Other Press, 2012.

Slote, Michael. *The Ethics of Care and Empathy*. London: Routledge, 2007.

Smelser, Neil J., and Richard Swedberg, eds. *The Handbook of Economic Sociology*. Princeton, NJ: Princeton University Press, 2005.

Smith, Rachel. "The Meaning of 'Free' Work: Service as a Gift, and Labor as a Commodity for Ni-Vanuatu Labor Migrants." In *Work, Society and the Ethical Self: Chimeras of Freedom in the Neoliberal Era*, edited by Chips Hann, 27–48. New York: Berghahn Books, 2021.

Smith, Robert Worthington. "Religious Influences in the Background of the British Labour Party." *The Southwestern Social Science Quarterly* 37, no. 4 (1957): 355–369.

Smithin, John N., ed. *What Is Money?*, vol. 6. London: Routledge, 2000.

Spencer, Stephen. *Theology Reforming Society: Revisiting Anglican Social Theology*. London: SCM Press, 2017.

Stackhouse, Max L., Peter J. Paris, Don S. Browning, and Diane Burdette Obenchain. *God and Gobalization*. 4 vols. Harrisburg, PA: Trinity Press International, 2000.

Standing, Guy. *The Precariat: The New Dangerous Class*. Rev. ed. London: Bloomsbury Academic, 2016.

Stark, Rodney, and Roger Finke. *Acts of Faith: Explaining the Human Side of Religion*. Berkeley: University of California Press, 2000.

Stimilli, Elettra. *Debt and Guilt: A Political Philosophy*. London: Bloomsbury Academic, 2019.

Stimilli, Elettra. *The Debt of the Living: Ascesis and Capitalism*. Albany, NY: SUNY Press, 2017.

Strathern, Marilyn. *Audit Cultures: Anthropological Studies in Accountability, Ethics, and the Academy*. European Association of Social Anthropologists. London: Routledge, 2000.

Swedberg, Richard. *Principles of Economic Sociology*. Princeton, NJ: Princeton University Press, 2003.

Tanner, Kathryn. *Christianity and the New Spirit of Capitalism*. New Haven, CT: Yale University Press, 2019.

Tanner, Kathryn. *Economy of Grace*. Minneapolis: Fortress Press, 2005.

Tanner, Kathryn. *Theories of Culture: A New Agenda for Theology*. Minneapolis, MN: Fortress Press, 1997.

Tawney, R. H. *Religion and the Rise of Capitalism: A Historical Study*. London: Verso, 2015.

Taylor, Charles. *A Secular Age*. Cambridge, MA: Belknap Press of Harvard University Press, 2007.

Testart, Alain. "The Extent and Significance of Debt Slavery." *Revue française de sociologie* 43 (2002): 173–204.

Thiem, Annika (Yannik). "Schmittian Shadows and Contemporary Theological-Political Constellations." *Social Research* 80, no. 1 (2013): 1–32.

Thompson, E. P. *The Making of the English Working Class*. New York: Pantheon, 1964.

Thompson, Randal Joy. *Proleptic Leadership on the Commons: Ushering in a New Global Order*. Bingley, UK: Emerald, 2020.

Tillich, Paul. *Theology of Culture*. New York: Oxford University Press, 1959.

Todeschini, Giacomo. *Les Marchands et le Temple: La société chrétienne et le cercle vertueux de la richesse du Moyen Âge à l'Epoque moderne*. Translated by Ida Giordano and Mathieu Arnoux. Paris: Albin Michel, 2017.

Todeschini, Giacomo. "Theological Roots of the Medieval/Modern Merchants' Self-Representation." In *The Self-Perception of Early Modern "Capitalists"*, edited by Margaret C. Jacob and Catherine Secretan, 17–46. New York: Palgrave-MacMillan, 2008.

Tonstad, Linn Marie. "Debt Time is Straight Time." *Political Theology* 17, no. 5 (2016): 434–448.

Tracy, David. *The Analogical Imagination: Christian Theology and the Culture of Pluralism*. New York: Crossroad, 1981.

Tribe, Keith. *Strategies of Economic Order: German Economic Discourse, 1750–1950*. Cambridge; New York: Cambridge University Press, 1995.

Tshaka, Rothney S. "On Being African and Reformed? Towards an African Reformed Theology Enthused by an Interlocution of Those on the Margins of Society." *HTS: Theological Studies* 70, no. 1 (2014): 1–7.

Turner, Victor. *The Ritual Process: Structure and Anti-Structure*. The Lewis Henry Morgan Lectures. Chicago: Aldine, 1969.

Vaca, Daniel. *Evangelicals Incorporated: Books and the Business of Religion in America*. Cambridge: Harvard University Press, 2019.

Viner, Jacob. *The Role of Providence in the Social Order: An Essay in Intellectual History*. Jayne Lectures for 1966, American Philosophical Society. Princeton, NJ: Princeton University Press, 1972.

Wariboko, Nimi. *Economics in Spirit and Truth: A Moral Philosophy of Finance*. New York: Palgrave Macmillan, 2014.

Wariboko, Nimi. *God and Money: A Theology of Money in a Globalizing World*. Lanham, MD: Lexington Books, 2008.

Wariboko, Nimi. *The Pentecostal Principle: Ethical Methodology in New Spirit*. Grand Rapids, MI: Eerdmans, 2012.

Wariboko, Nimi. *Split God: Pentecostalism and Critical Theory*. Albany: SUNY Press, 2018.

Warren, Rick. *The Purpose Driven Church: Growth Without Compromising Your Message & Mission*. Grand Rapids, MI: Zondervan, 1995.

Warren, Rick. *The Purpose-Driven Life: What on Earth am I Here For*? Grand Rapids, MI: Zondervan, 2002.

Waterman, Anthony M. C. *Political Economy and Christian Theology Since the Enlightenment: Essays in Intellectual History*. New York: Palgrave Macmillan, 2004.

Waterman, Anthony M. C. *Revolution, Economics and Religion: Christian Political Economy, 1798–1833*. Cambridge: Cambridge University Press, 1991.

Weber, Max. *Economy and Society: An Outline of Interpretive Sociology*. Berkeley: University of California Press, 1978.

Weber, Max. *The Protestant Ethic and the Spirit of Capitalism*. Translated by Stephen Kalberg. rev. and updated ed. New York: Oxford University Press, 2011.

Williams, Eric Eustace. *Capitalism and Slavery*. Chapel Hill, NC: University of North Carolina Press, 1944.

Winner, Lauren F. *The Dangers of Christian Practice: On Wayward Gifts, Characteristic Damage, and Sin*. New Haven, CT: Yale University press, 2018.

Winstanley, Gerrard, William Everard, John Palmer, and John Taylor. *The True Levellers Standard Advanced, or, The State of Community Opened, and Presented to the Sons of Men*. London 1649.

Woodmansee, Martha, and Mark Osteen, eds. *The New Economic Criticism: Studies at the Intersection of Literature and Economics*. New York: Routledge, 1999.

Wray, L. Randall, ed. *Credit and State Theories of Money: The Contributions of A. Mitchell Innes*. Northampton, MA: Edward Elgar, 2004.

Wray, L. Randall. *Modern Money Theory: A Primer on Macroeconomics for Sovereign Monetary Systems*. New York: Palgrave Macmillan, 2012.

Wurts, Kieryn E. "Neoliberalism and Political Theologies of the Post-Secular: Historical, Political, and Methodological Considerations in a 20th and 21st Century Discourse." *Religions* 12, no. 9 (2021): 680.

Wuthnow, Robert, ed. *Rethinking Materialism: Perspectives on the Spiritual Dimension of Economic Behavior*. Grand Rapids, MI: Eerdmans, 1995.

Wyschogrod, Edith, Jean-Joseph Goux, and Eric Boynton, eds. *The Enigma of Gift and Sacrifice*, Perspectives in Continental Philosophy. New York: Fordham University Press, 2002.

Yagi, Kiichiro. *Austrian and German Economic Thought*. New York: Routledge, 2010.

Youn, Chul Ho. "The Points and Tasks of Public Theology." *International Journal of Public Theology* 11 (2017): 64–87.

Yuengert, Andrew. "Roman Catholic Economics." In *The Oxford Handbook of Christianity and Economics*, edited by Paul Oslington, 153–76. New York: Oxford University Press, 2014.

Zaloom, Caitlin. "The Evangelical Financial Ethic: Doubled Forms and the Search for God in the Economic World." *American Ethnologist* 43, no. 2 (2016): 325–338.

Zelizer, Viviana A. *The Social Meaning of Money*. Princeton, NJ: Princeton University Press, 1997.